THE TASTE OF OUR TIME

Collection planned and directed by

ALBERT SKIRA

BIOGRAPHICAL AND CRITICAL STUDY
BY
ROBERT L. DELEVOY
Translated from the French by Stuart Gilbert

LÉGER

SKIRA

We are living in a dangerous and splendid age in which the end of a world and the beginnings of another are locked in a desperate embrace. But behind this troubled, calamitous foreground some timid flowers are springing from the tangled mass of decadent survivals and primitive achievements.

A New Space seems to be emerging, within which our young men in their twenties are in active quest of new directions, new viewpoints. What will come of it? The critical mind and the creative urge confront each other and no truce is given in the combat.

We have, I am convinced, to look back to the Middle Ages if we wish to find another age as dramatic as the one in which we now are living.

FERNAND LÉGER

CHRONOLOGICAL SURVEY

1881 Born February 4 at Argentan, Normandy. His father was a stock-breeder.

> 1889 Edison shows the first "motion pictures" at the Paris World's Fair.
> The Galerie des Machines (planned by the architect Dutert, built by the engineer Contamin) and the Eiffel Tower demonstrate the architectural applications of iron. Appearance of the first automobile driven by an internal combustion engine. With the linotype begins the age of industrial printing.

1890-1896 Studies at the municipal school of Argentan and at a religious school in the small town of Tinchebray.

> 1890 The French physiologist E. J. Marey invents a photographic plate for recording successive pictures of moving objects.
> C. von Ehrenfels enounces his theory of form.

> 1892 Horta builds the Hôtel Tassel, at Brussels, a striking illustration of the so-called Modern Style in architecture.
> Marey invents the first film projector.
> Lorentz discovers electrons.

> 1893 Invention of the Diesel engine.

> 1894 Anatole de Baudot inaugurates the use of concrete in large-scale edifices (church of Saint-Jean in Montmartre).

> 1895 The Russian physicist Popov makes the first experiments in wireless telegraphy. Edison and the Lumière brothers produce the first commercial cameras. Röntgen discovers X-rays.

> 1896 Georges Méliès sets up the first film studio at Montreuil, just outside Paris. At Brussels, Horta designs the Maison du Peuple, a new type of building with a structural framework of iron girders.

1897-1899 Léger studies architecture at Caen.

> 1897 Mackintosh designs the Glasgow School of Art. First successful flying machine built and tested by Clément Ader. Marconi opens the era of wireless telegraphy and founds in London the Wireless Telegraph and Signal Company.

> 1898 In England, Ebenezer Howard's book "Tomorrow" explores the possibilities of a new type of town: the garden city.

1900 **Léger goes to Paris where he finds employment as an architectural draughtsman.**

> 1900 Maurice Denis paints his "Homage to Cézanne." Derain and
> Vlaminck work together at Chatou. Picasso's first trip to Paris.
> Braque and Dufy come to Paris to study art.
> Gaudi builds the labyrinth in the Park Guëll at Barcelona.
> Triumph of the Modern Style ("art nouveau") at the Paris
> World's Fair.
> Planck formulates the quanta theory.
> Freud publishes "Die Traumdeutung."

> 1901 The first wireless message transmitted across the Atlantic.
> Inauguration of the Paris-Berlin automobile race.

1902 **Military service at Versailles (in the Engineers).**

> 1902 Picasso's first Paris exhibition, at the Berthe Weill Gallery.
> Méliès makes a film called "A Trip to the Moon."
> First performance of Debussy's opera "Pelléas et Mélisande."
> Perret employs concrete for building private houses.
> Van de Velde finishes building the Folkwang Museum at
> Hagen.
> Rutherford and Becquerel investigate radioactivity.

1903 **Admitted to the Ecole des Arts Décoratifs, Paris, but does not attend classes regularly. Fails the entrance examination at the Ecole des Beaux-Arts, but enters Gérôme's studio as an "élève libre," then moves on to Gabriel Ferrier's studio. Attends the Académie Julian.**

> 1903 Founding of the Salon d'Automne, Paris (Gauguin Retrospective).
> Matisse, Dufy, Friesz and Marquet exhibit at the Salon des
> Indépendants.
> The German Expressionists found the "Die Brücke" group
> at Dresden.
> The discoveries of Pierre Curie inaugurate the age of radioactive transformations.
> First flight of the Wright brothers at Dayton, Ohio.
> Berlage finishes building the Amsterdam Stock Exchange.
> Erection of the Ford automobile factory at Detroit.

1903-1905 **To earn a living, Léger works in an architect's office and, on the side, does retouching for a photographer. Shares a studio in the Avenue du Maine with a boyhood friend from Argentan, the painter André Mare. First paintings.**

1904 Picasso settles in Paris for good.
Matisse's first one-man show, at Vollard's.
Cézanne Room (42 canvases) at the Salon d'Automne.
Exhibition of French Primitives at the Pavillon de Marsan, Paris.
In Vienna, the architect Otto Wagner reacts against the Modern Style (Postsparkasse).
Pierre and Marie Curie awarded the Nobel Prize for physics for their discovery of radium; the Russian physiologist Pavlov awarded the Nobel Prize for medicine.

1905 Léger takes a studio in "La Ruche," Passage de Dantzig, in the Vaugirard district of Montparnasse.

1905 The Fauves create a sensation at the Salon d'Automne.
Seurat and Van Gogh retrospectives at the Indépendants.
First exhibition of the "Die Brücke" group at Dresden.
Hoffmann builds the Palais Stoclet at Brussels.
Lorentz, Einstein and Minkowski investigate the principle of relativity. Discovery of photons by Einstein.

1906 Goes through a difficult period in Paris. His health is bad and he spends the winter of 1905-1906 in Corsica, at Belgodere. Paints landscapes. Strongly influenced by Cézanne.

1906 Gauguin retrospective at the Salon d'Automne.
Bergson publishes "L'Evolution créatrice."
Baekeland produces the first synthetic resin, bakelite, a discovery heralding the present age of plastics.
Taxis and motor-driven buses make their appearance in the streets of Paris.

1907 Cézanne retrospective at the Salon d'Automne.
Picasso finishes "Les Demoiselles d'Avignon."
Auguste Lumière invents color photography.
In Germany, the Werkbund calls for an alliance of art and industry.

1908 His pictures being rejected by the jury of the Salon d'Automne, Braque exhibits them at Kahnweiler's.
Archipenko arrives in Paris.
Anton von Webern composes his "Passacaglia."
Worringer publishes "Abstraktion und Einfühlung."
First electronic tubes.

1909 Vigorous reaction against Impressionism. Paints "Woman Sewing." Meets Robert Delaunay and discovers the Douanier Rousseau.

1909 Marinetti's Futurist Manifesto published in the Figaro.
First performances of Diaghilev's Ballets Russes at the Châtelet Theater, Paris.
Schönberg publishes his "Harmonielehre" (1909-1911).
The Robie House, Chicago, designed by Frank Lloyd Wright, embodies a wholly original conception of organic architecture.
Behrens illustrates the possibilities of functional design in industrial architecture (A.E.G. Works, Berlin).
Blériot flies across the English Channel.
In New York, Gilbreth makes the first systematic study of forms in movement.

1910 The dealer D.H. Kahnweiler shows an interest in his work. Lives at 14, Avenue du Maine, then at 13, Rue de l'Ancienne-Comédie, where he begins painting the series of "Roofs." Works on "The Wedding."
Takes part, along with Delaunay, Gleizes, Le Fauconnier, André Mare, Picabia, Kupka, Marie Laurencin and Valensi, in the gatherings at Jacques Villon's that lead to the formation of the "Section d'Or" group.

1910 Picasso's portraits of Vollard, Kahnweiler and Uhde.
Manifesto of the Futurist Painters, signed at Milan (February 11) by Balla, Boccioni, Carrà, Russolo and Severini, published in "Comoedia" (May 18).
In Berlin, Herwarth Walden launches the review "Der Sturm" (March 3); contributors include Apollinaire, Aragon, Arp, Boccioni, Breton, Cendrars, Delaunay, Eluard, Freud, Kandinsky, Kokoschka, Léger, Loos, Marc, Marinetti, Moholy-Nagy, Pechstein, Schwitters and Tzara.
Stravinsky's "Fire Bird" performed in Paris by Diaghilev's Ballets Russes.
In Vienna, Loos refines the plan and structure of the dwelling-house (Steiner House).
Founding of the Austrian Werkbund.
The Frank Lloyd Wright exhibition in Berlin opens Europe to the influence of the Chicago school of architecture.

1910-1913 Bertrand Russell and Alfred Whitehead publish their "Principia Mathematica," a pioneer work in symbolic logic.

1911 "Nudes in the Forest" creates a sensation at the Salon des Indépendants. Paints "The Smokers." Exhibits with Delaunay, Gleizes, Le Fauconnier, La Fresnaye, Metzinger, and Marie Laurencin at the eighth exhibition of the Brussels Independents.

1911 Takes part in the first Section d'Or exhibition, with Villon, Kupka, La Fresnaye, Metzinger and Picabia, and in the second exhibition of the Société Normande de Peinture Moderne (Galerie d'Art Contemporain, Rue Tronchet, Paris). Collaborates with La Fresnaye, Duchamp-Villon and Rouault in the presentation of a "dining room" and a "study" designed by André Mare for the Salon d'Automne.

1911 Cubist exhibitions at the Salon des Indépendants (Room 41) and Salon d'Automne (Room 8) attract wide attention.
Klee's first one-man show at Munich.
Gropius promotes the use of glass screens in industrial architecture (Fagus Works, Alfeld).
Husserl publishes "Ideen zu einer reinen Phänomenologie."

1912 Exhibits "Woman in Blue" at the Salon d'Automne and "The Smokers" at the Indépendants. First one-man show at Kahnweiler's. Takes part in the second Section d'Or exhibition, in the Salon de Juin organized by the Société Normande de Peinture Moderne, in a cubist exhibition at Barcelona (Dalmau Gallery), and in the "Knave of Diamonds" exhibition organized in Moscow by Malevitch.

1912 Delaunay begins his series of "Windows." Mondrian and Malevitch come to Paris. Beginnings of Synthetic Cubism. First Futurist exhibition in Paris (Bernheim Gallery).
In his "Pierrot Lunaire" Schönberg breaks with the tonal system. Rutherford's experiments on the structure of atoms.

1913 Moves into a studio at 86, Rue Notre-Dame-des-Champs, in Montparnasse. Signs a contract with Kahnweiler. Paints the series of "Variations of Forms." Exhibits at the first Herbstsalon in Berlin. Delivers a lecture at the Académie Wassilieff, Paris (May 5), on "The Origins of Contemporary Painting and its Representative Value."

1913 Delaunay paints "Simultaneous Disks." Apollinaire publishes "Les Peintres cubistes." Canudo launches the review "Montjoie." Malevitch produces the first suprematist painting. Tatlin and Rodchenko found Constructivism.
The Armory Show in New York, an international exhibition of modern art with 1100 works by over 300 artists.
First performance of Stravinsky's "Rite of Spring" in Paris.
Niels Bohr's theory of circumferences. The first assembly line goes into operation at the Ford Plant in Detroit.

1914 Delivers a lecture at the Académie Wassilieff (May 9) on "Present-day Achievements in Painting." Paints "The Fourteenth of July." Mobilized on August 2. Takes part in the fighting in the Argonne (1914-1916) and serves as a stretcher-bearer at Verdun (1916-1917).

1914 Marcel Duchamp's first "ready-mades." Manifesto of Futurist Architecture. Mondrian's first neo-plastic paintings.
Chaplin's first films. Van de Velde builds the Werkbund exhibition theater at Cologne.

1915 Malevitch issues the Suprematist Manifesto. Arp exhibits his first abstract works at Zurich.

1916 On leave in Paris, Léger is taken by Apollinaire to see Chaplin's films. Gassed in September on the Verdun front.

1916 Freyssinet designs the hangars at Orly, Frank Lloyd Wright the Hotel Imperial in Tokyo.
Chaplin makes "The Fireman." Feuillade produces "Judex."

1917 Under treatment at the Villepinte hospital. Discharged from the army at the end of the year.
"The Card Party" marks a turning point in the evolution of his art and of his whole conception of painting.

1917 At Leyden, Van Doesburg and Mondrian launch the review "De Stijl" (1917-1932).
Opening of the Dada Gallery in Zurich.
Chaplin makes "The Tramp."

1918 Paints "Acrobats" and "Disks" and does illustrations for "J'ai tué" by Blaise Cendrars.

1918 Death of Apollinaire.
Le Corbusier and Ozenfant publish the purist manifesto, "Après le Cubisme."
Signing of the Armistice (November 11).

1919 Paints "The City," "The Typographer" and "Mechanical Elements." Illustrations for "La fin du monde, filmée par l'ange Notre-Dame" by Blaise Cendrars.
Marries Jeanne Lohy (December 2).

1919 Mondrian returns to Paris (where he remains until 1939).
Max Ernst's first collages.
Gropius founds the Weimar Bauhaus.
Marcel Proust awarded the Prix Goncourt for "A l'ombre des jeunes filles en fleurs."
Wiene and Lang shoot "The Cabinet of Dr Caligari."

1920 Léger meets Le Corbusier.

> 1920 The Dadaists produce the first photomontages. Moholy-Nagy and Man Ray elevate the photogram to the status of a means of artistic expression. Ozenfant and Le Corbusier launch the review "L'Esprit Nouveau" (1920-1925). Mondrian's book "Le Néoplasticisme" published in Paris by Léonce Rosenberg. Kahnweiler publishes "Der Weg zum Kubismus" in Munich. Klee appointed to a professorship at the Bauhaus.
> First radio broadcasts.
> Chaplin makes "The Kid."

1921 Works with Blaise Cendrars on the motion picture "La Roue" produced by Abel Gance. Signs "Le Grand Déjeuner" and illustrates André Malraux's "Lunes en papier." First contacts with the "De Stijl" painters, Van Doesburg and Mondrian.

> 1921 Severini publishes "Du Cubisme au Classicisme." In conjunction with the Bauhaus, Van Doesburg founds a De Stijl group at Weimar. Viking Eggeling and Hans Richter make the first abstract films. Van de Velde designs the Kröller-Müller Museum, Otterlo (Holland).
> In "Space, Time and Gravitation" the English astronomer and physicist A. S. Eddington studies the problem of the universe from a new angle.
> Einstein awarded the Nobel Prize for physics.

1922 On his mother's death, Léger inherits a farm at Lisores (Normandy) where from now on he makes frequent stays. Moves to Fontenay-aux-Roses, just outside Paris. Finishes "Woman and Child." Commissioned to design the curtain, sets and costumes for the Swedish ballet "Skating Rink" (music by Honegger).

> 1922 Kandinsky and Moholy-Nagy appointed professors at the Bauhaus. Moholy-Nagy and L. Kassak publish the "Buch neuer Künstler" (with reproductions of works by Léger, Picasso, Malevitch, Schwitters, Le Corbusier and others).
> J. J. P. Oud designs the "De Unie" restaurant at Rotterdam. Niels Bohr awarded the Nobel Prize for physics for his work on the structure of the atom.

1923 Designs sets and costumes for "La Création du Monde" (music by Darius Milhaud, scenario by Blaise Cendrars). Collaborates with Mallet-Stevens, Cavalcanti and Claude Autant-Lara in designing sets and costumes for the film "L'inhumaine" produced by Marcel L'Herbier.

1923 Le Corbusier publishes "Vers une architecture." De Stijl exhibition in Paris (Galerie L'Effort Moderne). Schwitters launches the review "Merz." Auguste Perret designs the church at Le Raincy, Le Corbusier the Maison La Roche at Auteuil (both in the Paris suburbs).
Louis de Broglie lays down the principles of wave mechanics.

1924 Léger, Ozenfant, Marie Laurencin and Exter join in giving free art classes. Plans and directs "Ballet Mécanique," the first film without a scenario (photography by Man Ray and Dudley Murphy, music by George Antheil).
Trip to Italy with Léonce Rosenberg; visits Ravenna.

1924 With Kandinsky, Feininger and Jawlensky, Klee founds the group known as "Die Blauen Vier."
André Breton issues the Surrealist Manifesto.
Picasso does sets for "Mercure" (music by Erik Satie).
Rietveld's architectural design influenced by Neo-Plasticism.
Gershwin makes a hit in New York with "Rhapsody in Blue."

1925 At the Exhibition of Decorative Arts, Paris, Léger decorates the entrance hall of the "Ambassade Française" pavilion (with Delaunay) and executes his first murals for Le Corbusier in the "Esprit Nouveau" pavilion. Lectures at the Collège de France on "The Aesthetics of the Machine."

1925 First group exhibition of the Surrealists, Galerie Pierre, Paris.
The Bauhaus moves from Weimar to Dessau.
New films: "The Battleship Potemkin" (Eisenstein), "La Marche des Machines" (Deslaw), "The Gold Rush" (Chaplin), "The Joyless Street" (Pabst).

1926 Exhibits at the Galerie des Quatre Chemins, Paris.

1926 First Klee exhibition in Paris.
Kandinsky publishes "Punkt und Linie zu Fläche."
Beginnings of experimental television.

1927 Zervos founds "Les Cahiers d'Art."
Neutra designs a sanatorium at Los Angeles, Brinkmann and Van der Vlugt the Van Nelle Works at Rotterdam, Moser the St. Antonskirche at Basel.
Heidegger publishes "Sein und Zeit."
"The Jazz Singer," the first sound film produced in the United States.
Lindbergh crosses the Atlantic in the "Spirit of St. Louis."

1928 Trip to Berlin for the opening of his one-man show at the Flechtheim Gallery (100 items). Gives a lecture there, centering on Le Corbusier and entitled "Actualités."

1928 André Breton publishes "Le Surréalisme et la Peinture." Success of the Diaghilev ballet "Apollon musagète" (music by Stravinsky).
Dial telephones and sound films make their appearance in France.
Dali and Bunuel produce "Un Chien andalou."
Founding of the Congrès Internationaux d'Architecture Moderne (C.I.A.M.) in Switzerland.
First exhibition of Rational Architecture in Rome.
Poelzig builds the I. G. Farben plant at Frankfort.
Einstein formulates his unified field theory, Heisenberg his principle of uncertainty ("Unbestimmtheitsrelation").

1929 Teaches at the Académie Moderne with Ozenfant.

1929 International Exhibition of Abstract Art at Zurich. Founding of the Museum of Modern Art, New York. Mies van der Rohe designs the German pavilion at the Barcelona World's Fair.
Le Corbusier designs the Villa Savoye at Passy.
The Nobel Prize for physics awarded to Louis de Broglie.
Heidegger publishes "Vom Wesen des Grundes," Husserl his "Logische Untersuchungen."
Leduc takes out the first patent for jet propulsion.

1930 Léger meets Calder.

1930 Moholy-Nagy devises his first "Space Modulators" in London. Klee teaches at the Düsseldorf Academy. Death of the Russian poet Mayakovsky.

1931 Summer stay on the Lake of Constance (July-August). First trip to the United States (September-December); visits New York and Chicago.

1931 New films: "City Lights" (Chaplin), "The Threepenny Opera" (Pabst), "Le Sang du Poète" (Cocteau), "Le Million" (René Clair).
Gaston Baty makes his début at the Théâtre Montparnasse.
Construction of Rockefeller Center, New York.
Anderson discovers the positive electron.
European financial crisis.

1932 Teaches at the Académie de la Grande-Chaumière, Paris. Trip to Sweden and Norway.

1932 Formation in Paris of the "Abstraction-Création" group. First Paris exhibition of Calder's "mobiles." The Bauhaus moves from Dessau to Berlin. Le Corbusier designs the Swiss Pavilion at the Cité Universitaire, Paris. René Clair produces "A Nous la Liberté." Paul Eluard publishes "La Vie immédiate."
Discovery of the neutron by the English physicist Sir James Chadwick.
Birth of electronic optics.

1933 Trips to Zurich, for the opening of his exhibition at the Kunsthaus, and Greece (with Le Corbusier) for a C.I.A.M. Congress. On the way back to Paris, gives a lecture on shipboard on the theme "L'Architecture devant la Vie."

1933 The Bauhaus closed down by the Nazis. Klee returns to Bern, Kandinsky settles in Paris. In Paris, Albert Skira launches the review "Minotaure" (1933-1939). Elie Faure publishes "La Vie des Formes." Artificial production of radioactivity by Joliot-Curie. Nobel Prize for physics awarded to the Austrian scientist Erwin Schrödinger for his work on the atom.
Discovery of the photoelectric cell.

**1934 Spends the summer at Antibes (July). Goes to London in August to design sets for Alexander Korda's film "The Shape of Things to Come" based on the book by H. G. Wells.
Trip to Stockholm in September, where he exhibits at the Modern Gallery. The Göteborg Museum buys his "Woman at her Toilette." Lecture at the Sorbonne, "From the Acropolis to the Eiffel Tower."**

1934 First exhibition of "Machine Art" at the Museum of Modern Art, New York.
Gaston Bachelard publishes "Le nouvel esprit scientifique."

1935 Decorates the Hall of Physical Culture at the Brussels Fair. Second trip to the United States in September with Le Corbusier. Exhibits at the Museum of Modern Art, New York, and at the Art Institute of Chicago.

1935 Schwitters leaves Germany and settles in Norway.
Le Corbusier publishes "La Ville radieuse."

1936 Frank Lloyd Wright designs the "Falling Water" house at Bear Run, Pa.
First practical applications of the electronic microscope by the biologist Marton.
Spanish Civil War. Picasso appointed Director of the Prado by the Republicans.

1937 Sets for the ballet "David Triomphant" produced by Serge Lifar at the Paris Opera (music by Rieti). Designs scenery for the Fête des Syndicats at the Vélodrome d'Hiver, Paris. Mural painting ("Le Transport des Forces") for the Palais de la Découverte. Lectures at Antwerp on "Color in the World" (November). Goes to Finland for his exhibition at the Artek Gallery, Helsinki, where he makes friends with A. Aalto.

1937 Picasso paints "Guernica" for the Spanish Pavilion at the Paris World's Fair.
Le Corbusier publishes "Quand les cathédrales étaient blanches."
Moholy-Nagy founds the New Bauhaus in Chicago (now Chicago Institute of Design). Opening of the Museum of Non-Objective Painting, New York. Gropius appointed head of the Harvard School of Architecture.
Construction of the Ministry of National Education and Health at Rio de Janeiro, finished in 1943 (architects: Costa, Niemeyer, Reidy, Leao, Moreira).

1938 Summer holiday at Vézelay with Le Corbusier (August). Third trip to the United States (September 1938 to March 1939). Decorates the New York apartment of Nelson A. Rockefeller, Jr. Stays at Provincetown with John Dos Passos and on Long Island with the architect Harrison. Gives a course of eight lectures at Yale on "Color in Architecture."

1938 International Surrealist Exhibition in Paris.
Jean Renoir's film "La Grande Illusion."
Karl Jaspers publishes "Existenzphilosophie."
First use of fluorescent lighting.
First electronic calculating machine, designed by Howard Aikin.

1939 Sets for J. R. Bloch's play "La Naissance d'une Cité," performed at the Vélodrome d'Hiver, Paris (music by Darius Milhaud and Arthur Honegger).

1939 Delaunay organizes the first Salon des Réalités Nouvelles, Paris.
Splitting of the atom.
Outbreak of the Second World War.

1940-1944 In October 1940 Léger sails from Marseilles for the United States. Teaches at Yale University, with Darius Milhaud, Henri Focillon and André Maurois. Friendship with Father Couturier. Also teaches at Mills College, Oakland, Calif. Period of "Divers" and "Cyclists."

Exhibits at Paul Rosenberg's, New York, in 1942. The same year, at the Pierre Matisse Gallery in New York, he meets most of the exiles from the Paris art world: Masson, Tanguy, Matta, Breton, Zadkine, Ernst, Chagall, Mondrian, Ozenfant. In 1944 he composes the sequence "La fille au cœur fabriqué" for Hans Richter's film "Dreams That Money Can Buy."

1940 Paris: artists are dispersed and museums closed.
Mondrian arrives in the United States, Schwitters in England.
Rolls-Royce jet engine developed by Frank Whittle.

1941 Breton, Chagall and Ernst arrive in the United States.
Discovery of plutonium by Glenn T. Seaborg of the University of California.

1942 Le Corbusier writes "La Maison des Hommes."
Release of atomic energy achieved by a group of American physicists under Enrico Fermi.

1944 Picasso retrospective at the Salon d'Automne, Paris.
Pollock, Motherwell and Baziotes exhibit in New York.

1945 Léger exhibitions at the Fogg Art Museum, Cambridge, Mass., and in New York (Valentine Gallery and Kootz Gallery). Returns to France in December.

1945 Merleau-Ponty publishes "Phénoménologie de la Perception."

1946 Exhibits his American paintings at the Carré Gallery, Paris. Commissioned by Father Couturier to design a mosaic for the façade of the church at Assy (Haute-Savoie). Delivers a lecture at the Sorbonne.

1946 Opening of the Musée Picasso at Antibes.
In Paris, Fougeron heads the movement in favor of Socialist Realism. The younger generation of constructivist painters (Dewasne, Deyrolle, Vasarely) and the first "informal" painters (Wols, Fautrier) appear on the scene.

1947 Spends the summer in Normandy. "Portrait of Paul Eluard." Hans Richter's film "Dreams That Money Can Buy," produced in collaboration with Léger, Calder, Duchamp, Ernst and Man Ray, wins a prize at the Venice Film Festival.

1948 Sets for the ballet "Le Pas d'Acier" (music by Prokofiev). Trip to Poland for the Peace Congress at Wroclaw (Breslau). Léger and Jean Bazaine deliver a joint lecture at Brussels, in dialogue form, on "The Art of Today."

1948 Neutra designs the Villa Tremaine at Montecito, California.
Invention of the transistor.
The mathematician Norbert Wiener defines the principles of
cybernetics.

**1949 Léger produces his first ceramics, at Biot (Alpes-Maritimes).
Retrospective exhibition (1905-1949) at the Musée d'Art
Moderne, Paris.
Designs sets for Darius Milhaud's opera "Bolivar."**

1949 Chagall's first ceramics. Le Corbusier begins the construction
of an apartment house at Marseilles. New methods of producing sounds: Pierre Schaeffer makes the first experiments in
concrete music in Paris; Werner Meyer-Eppler and Herbert
Eimart found the first studio of electronic music at Cologne.

**1950 Death of Madame Léger. Sets up a ceramic workshop at Biot.
Exhibits at the Tate Gallery, London (catalogue preface by
Douglas Cooper). Mosaic for the American Memorial at
Bastogne. Paints "The Constructors." Present at the conse-
cration of the Church of Assy (Haute-Savoie).**

1950 Wall paintings and mosaics by Severini for the University of
Fribourg (Switzerland). Einstein's second theory of relativity.
Bertrand Russell awarded the Nobel Prize for Literature.

**1951 On January 20 a diocesan commission on sacred art approves
the seventeen designs for stained-glass windows made by
Léger for the church at Audincourt (Doubs). Exhibits his first
polychrome sculptures at the Louise Leiris Gallery, Paris.
Executes a vast decorative composition for the French Pavilion
at the Milan Triennale.**

1951 Picasso paints "Massacre in Korea."
Inauguration of the Chapel of the Rosary designed and deco-
rated by Matisse for the Dominican Convent at Vence, on the
French Riviera.

**1952 Elected a corresponding member of the Académie Royale
Flamande des Sciences, des Lettres et des Beaux-Arts de
Belgique. Gives a lecture at the Kunsthalle, Bern (April 10),
on "Architecture and Color." Exhibits at the Antibes Museum.
Goes to Venice for the 26th Biennale. Marries his pupil Nadine
Khodessevitch and settles at Gif-sur-Yvette (Seine-et-Oise).
Mural panel for the United Nations Building, New York.
Sets and costumes for a Janine Charrat ballet performed at
Amboise for the 500th anniversary of the birth of Leonardo
da Vinci.**

1952 Picasso paints "War and Peace." Death of Paul Eluard. Pierre Schaeffer publishes "A la recherche d'une musique concrète."

1953 Landscapes in the Seine-et-Oise countryside around Gif-sur-Yvette. Exhibits more polychrome sculptures at the Louis Carré Gallery, Paris. Léger exhibition at the Museum of Modern Art, New York. Illustrations for Paul Eluard's poem "Liberté." Gives a lecture on "Modern Painting" at Brussels.

1953 Frank Lloyd Wright designs the Solomon R. Guggenheim Museum, New York. Gaston Bachelard publishes "Le Matérialisme rationnel."
Olivier Messiaen composes "Le Réveil des Oiseaux."

1954 Designs windows for the church at Courfaivre (Switzerland) and the University of Caracas (Venezuela). "The Country Outing" and "The Great Parade" stand out among his recent works exhibited at the Maison de la Pensée Française, Paris. Colored study for the Memorial Hospital at Saint-Lô (architect, Nelson). Plans a mosaic composition for the auditorium of the São Paulo Opera, Brazil (architect, Oscar Niemeyer).

1954 Death of Matisse. Death of the critic Maurice Raynal. Diffusion of the theories of the Russian geneticist Lysenko. The first atomic power station goes into operation in the U.S.S.R. (June 27).

**1955 Awarded the Grand Prize at the São Paulo Biennale. Retrospective exhibition at the Lyons Museum. Produces a sculpture, a ceramic panel and a mosaic for the coking plant of "Gaz de France," at Alfortville, in the suburbs of Paris. Trip to Czechoslovakia for the Sokol Congress at Prague.
Dies at Gif-sur-Yvette, August 17, aged 74.**

1955 Deaths of Baumeister, Hofer, Pechstein and Tanguy. Death of Albert Einstein.
Le Corbusier finishes the church of Notre-Dame-du-Haut at Ronchamp (Haute-Savoie).
The U.S. Navy launches the first atomic submarine.

**1956 Inauguration of the Memorial Hospital at Saint-Lô. Large-scale Léger Retrospective Exhibition at the Musée des Arts Décoratifs, Paris (222 items).
Publication of Léger's "Mes Voyages," with a poem by Aragon.**

1957 Laying of the foundation stone of the Fernand Léger Museum at Biot (Alpes-Maritimes), on February 24. The official opening of the museum takes place on May 13, 1960.

SELF-PORTRAIT, 1904-1905. MADAME ANDRÉ MARE COLLECTION, PARIS.

OUTSET OF A GREAT ADVENTURE

An Insatiable Curiosity

> We had better stop calling ourselves artists and leave that lustrous appellation to pedicures and hairdressers.
>
> ERIK SATIE

A DRASTIC revaluation of values has been taking place in present-day France and its tone is set by the work of such avant-garde writers as Henri Michaux, René Char and Alain Robbe-Grillet. On the speculative level, polyvalence, quanta, anti logic and information theory are the order of the day. On the material plane we live in a world of jets and concrete music, transistors, images that blast our eyes, the stridences of speed, electronic gadgets and plastics, Oceanian masks and Oriental calligrams. Naturally enough, the painting born of this universal flux makes much of discontinuous, dynamic ,"open" figurations timed to the feverish rhythms of modern life, and has established a new order of values in the world of art.

Already we feel that Léger belongs to another age. This Norman peasant with the build of a stevedore, addict of fullbodied wine, wild flowers, automobile races, buxom girls, factories and high-tension pylons, also liked tinkering with crystal sets and new inventions. He lived in the age of the silent movie, dodecaphonal music, the Russian Ballet, steam locomotives, propellers, push bicycles, cannons and steel, biplanes and "colonial art." He found all the "truth" he needed in the poems of his friend Blaise Cendrars, and unfailing satisfaction in the profoundly human warmth and humor of Charlie Chaplin's films.

It was in Paris, in 1900, when he was just under twenty, that Fernand Léger tried his hand at painting. The first hint of his vocation had come to him in his schooldays, when he had amused himself *sub rosa* making cruel caricatures of his cassocked teachers. That "glorious brute," his father, had died when his small son was still wrestling with the ABC. "If he'd lived some years longer, I'd have been, like him, a cattle dealer, that's certain. I was a hefty kid and kept my muscles in good trim. There's a physical side to the life of the stock-breeder that would surely have appealed to me."[1]

When he was sixteen his mother, "a poor, priest-ridden soul," and an uncle (his guardian) arranged for him to study under an architect at Caen. Later he was provided with funds enabling him to complete his training in Paris. But quite soon he decided, not without qualms of conscience, to abandon architecture and replace the drawing pen with brush and pencil. As he used to tell his friends in later years, he was "a restless sort of bloke." "I had to be pushed by circumstances," he added, "if I was to make anything of myself."[2] In the event, the classes he attended, off and on, at the Ecole des Beaux-Arts did far less to mobilize his hand and eye than did the cultural, political and social changes that took place in the western world during the early decades of the century. When he died, in 1955, in full activity (he was planning a series of gigantic compositions on the "Fourteenth of July" theme), he had come to be regarded as *par excellence* the painter of an epoch, that of the pioneers of modern art, of Le Corbusier, Braque, Darius Milhaud and Picasso; of those eventful years when the tastes, the sensibility, and even the way of seeing of a whole generation were being profoundly modified. This makes it all the more surprising that today his work finds favor with only a relatively small, if fervent, group of admirers.

MY MOTHER'S GARDEN, 1905. MUSÉE FERNAND LÉGER, BIOT.

True, Léger's œuvre is charged with a rugged power, an exuberance of forms and plastic values and a stark violence that tend even today to jar on over-sensitive eyes; yet surely it should have been recognized long ago for what it is: the work of a giant in artistic stature. For, paradoxically enough, this art has failed to make good with the public at large, despite the fact that for twenty years (1920-1940) it exercised a vital, if indirect, influence, by way of theater sets, posters, window displays, typography and the tectonics of book production. It might be suggested, perhaps, that such indirect influences should not be taken over-seriously, since they concern merely decorative—hence super-ficial, not to say trivial—factors. But any such view would be totally mistaken; in the fullest sense of the term Léger is a great creative artist. His contribution to the art of today was of prime importance, even if it has ceased to activate "modern" trends ("modern" does not necessarily mean contemporaneous). To persist in ignoring the greatness of Léger's art and its claim on the collective consciousness, simply because its content is veiled beneath an exterior aspect that is harsh, rugged, elemental, ponderous, would be to garble the true scale of artistic values. An agile eye can readily adjust its focus to the angularity and spareness of Léger's world of forms, and this forceful record of the visual and emotive experiences of a great artist may justly rank as an outstanding manifestation of the period with which it is bound up so closely.

Conscious of the deficiency of his cultural equipment, and unsure as yet of his path, Léger made a cautious start. Of his early works only a few of the pictures executed in 1904-1905, in which he still kept to the traditional way of seeing, have survived. These include the powerful *Self-Portrait* (Madame André Mare Collection, Paris); *My Mother's Garden* (Fernand Léger Museum, Biot), painted at Argentan in small touches of green, blue and pink; the *Portrait of the Artist's Uncle* (Biot), painted with a full brush in rather strident tones. These minor works, gently toying with the motif, are little more than brief notations. Forms are unclearly rendered and both technique and execution betray a certain lack of confidence.[3] There can be little doubt, however, that the exhibition of forty-two canvases by Cézanne at the 1904 Salon d'Automne opened up new horizons to the young artist. In any case he was enough impressed by it to set to painting in the winter of 1905-1906, in Corsica, a number of schematic, architecturally ordered landscapes on geometric lines. In the *Corsican Village at Sunset* (1905, Mouradian and Valloton Collection, Paris), we have a curious anticipation of the Spanish landscapes Picasso was to paint in 1909 at Horta de Ebro in, needless to say, a much more accomplished style and with a finer economy of means.

"No sooner had I made these landscapes," Léger tells us, "than I felt a distaste for Impressionism. But I could only react against the impressionist tendencies in my own work and I took this course because I felt that the art of the Impressionists had been instinctively harmonious, in keeping with its age, whereas my age had ceased to be harmonious. However, I had to pass through this phase, nothing comes as a 'bolt from the blue,' everything hangs together."[4]

Signs of this reaction can be seen even in the admirable *Studies of Nudes* (1905-1908, Biot) in Indian ink, in which the young artist shows an amazing facility, a feeling for attitudes and synthetic form, and whose deft, concise, significant line is rich in promise for the future.

TABLE AND FRUIT, 1909. THE COLLECTION OF THE MINNEAPOLIS INSTITUTE
OF ARTS, THE WILLIAM HOOD DUNWOODY FUND, 1947.

AT THE ANTIPODES OF IMPRESSIONISM

The Ascendancy of Cézanne

> The very first painting struck deep into the
> future. And each successive work modifies,
> illuminates, confirms, exalts and re-creates, or
> pre-creates, all the others.
>
> MAURICE MERLEAU-PONTY

LÉGER had been impervious to the sound and fury of the avant-garde and the sensational incursion of the Fauves at the 1905 Salon d'Automne had left him cold. For at this time he was preoccupied exclusively with "finding himself" in the fullest sense. He had plunged into a flood of experiments and projects. And he made no secret of his devotion to Cézanne, in whom he spontaneously recognized the true "primitive of a new art." "Cézanne," he said, "is an instinctive; he has an open mind and his painting's always stimulating and suggestive. That's the difference between him and Renoir. Renoir's art is closed, self-contained. You can copy him, but that's all you can do. You can't get a man like that out of your system."[5]

Let there be no mistake. What Léger learned from his study of the most happily inspired creations of the master of the Montagne Sainte-Victoire was far more than the elements of a personal language. He trained his eye and in so doing developed a way of seeing that largely dispensed with the yardsticks of conventional art and figural traditions of the past. *Table and Fruit* (1909, Minneapolis), his first wholly successful work, reveals a thorough-going, passionate assimilation of the Cézannesque *ars poetica.* Here the classical structure of the still life, centered on an axis, is disrupted; table, fruit and dish move freely in an unstable frame of reference having no fixed dimensions; objects are disintegrated and reduced to the condition of plastic signs, modulated within a color dimension.

Could Léger continue to exploit so fascinating a heritage, without running the risk of succumbing completely to its influence? In any case he quickly realized that the fluid forms, the subtle play of colors, the translucences, the imponderables and fundamental elasticity of Cézanne's pictorial architecture could not wholly satisfy his instinctual urge to stiffen and consolidate his forms, to handle them (as he said) "without a trace of sentimentality" and to face up to the problem of volumes. Yet it is evident that he bore in mind the master's famous dictum, that "everything in nature is modeled in terms of the sphere, the cone and the cylinder," when he painted the figure of the *Woman Sewing* (1909), inspired by a familiar attitude of his mother's.

Despite its obvious shortcomings, this canvas marks the beginning of Léger's truly creative work. Taciturn, experimental and dogmatic, it inaugurates a method of approach that was destined to persist throughout the artist's career. Here all life is arrested in a ruthlessly inert formal structure, the human figure is depersonalized and treated as an object pure and simple, like a machine-made effigy composed of joints and rigid parts dovetailed into a solid block. Technically speaking, this work has a singular ambivalence and combines two contrasting modes of presentation; though the painter seems to be toying with chiaroscuro and effects of foreshortening, he peremptorily discards classical modeling and any hint of material depth, and replaces them with tight-drawn planes that look like strips of sheet metal folded into angular ridges. His desire to render volumes led Léger to embark on a strange venture, purely personal and absolutely independent of that other venture which

WOMAN SEWING, 1909. PRIVATE COLLECTION, PARIS.

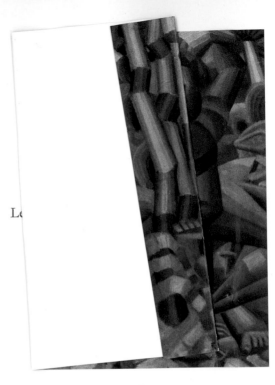

NUDES IN THE FOREST, 1909-1910. RIJKSMUSEUM KRÖLLER-MÜLLER, OTTERLO (HOLLAND).

had now brought Cubism to its crucial phase; for this was the very time when Picasso was completing, at the Bateau-Lavoir, his *Portrait of Ambroise Vollard*. A comparison of the two pictures reveals the fundamental differences between the art of the Montmartre intellectuals and that of the down-to-earth "peasant" of Montparnasse who when, in the following year, he had his first view of "orthodox" cubist art, remarked: "These fellows move on the heights and haven't any foothold

on mother earth. Personally, I pick up all I want in the street."
He had already "picked up" fragments of corrugated iron, metal
tubes and builders' debris—all that was needed to orient his
sensibility. In the street, too, he rubbed shoulders with the workers, for he relished the company of the artisan who laughs and
sings in his off hours. He had taken his social bearings, and his
philosophy of life was no less simple and forthright. And he now
made no secret of his purpose: that of creating a type of art
"at the antipodes of Impressionism."

In the course of painting the *Woman Sewing*, his desire for a
solid structural schema incited him to embark on an ambitious
program. This was to consolidate and make clear his previous
discoveries, and to test his architectonic sense and capacity for
ordered composition. This program he carried out with complete
success in that masterwork, *Nudes in the Forest* (1909-1910,
Kröller-Müller Museum, Otterlo), which has the same place
and role in Léger's œuvre as the *Demoiselles d'Avignon* (1907) in
Picasso's. All in opaque, muted tones, this large canvas is per-
vaded through and through with a subdued, intermittent har-
mony, based on a cold dominant. The naked bodies of the woodmen have a purplish sheen, the forest and its ruins are grey,
tinged with greenish blue and dappled here and there with
near-white patches. This picture seems like a vision of another
planet, a Martian landscape, with its apocalyptic medley of crude
forms, truncated cones, cylindrical mandrels, dislocated bodies.
There is an affinity, indeed an osmosis, between human elements
—torsos, legs and arms—and the segments of a tree trunk cut
up into billets. In this extraordinary composition, with its
clashes of forms (reminding us of the clashes of words in Blaise
Cendrars' poems), Léger's disjunction of objects into scattered
parts is far from haphazard; the dynamic tension of skillfully
planned contrasts both reassembles the *disjecta membra*, and
permeates the picture surface with strange, pulsating rhythms.

THREE FIGURES, 1910-1911. MILWAUKEE ART CENTER.

A NEW MODE OF SEEING

Forms in Movement

I perceived that it was a truly salutary and
honorable thing for a man to be, during his
sojourn here below, something of a sweeper
of the earth.

CLAUDE DE SAINT-MARTIN

REALITY has been broken up into large loose parts, then put
together again on an assembly line. Hence the metamor-
phosis it has undergone in our generation, and the new mystique
of the machine, in terms of which a faceless wood-cutter links
the mechanized world with the world of nature. Treated on the
same lines as the forest trees and performing their routine tasks
with the precision of an internal combustion engine, Léger's
woodmen give the impression of themselves being things of
cylinders and pistons, and their gestures have an automatism
corresponding to the tempo and the dynamism of the machine
age. Contemplated thus from a new angle, the traditional image
of man takes on a dubious look and all the familiar ways of
seeing lose their comfortable certitude.

That little known work, *Three Figures* (1910-1911), all trace
of which was lost from the time when it figured near Marcel
Duchamp's *Nude descending a Staircase* at the Armory Show in
New York (1913) until its recent acquisition by the Milwaukee
Art Center, is a further confirmation of the discipline the painter
was imposing on himself. But it also marks a new phase in the
evolution of his art: his refusal to indulge in any "picturesque"

THE WEDDING, 1911. MUSÉE NATIONAL D'ART MODERNE, PARIS.

depiction that countenanced the supposedly stable values of a still recent past. For Léger felt instinctively that the conventional methods of rendering optical data failed to provide the means of setting forth his personal experience; what he now was aiming at was to suggest movement in terms of the geometrical vocabulary of forms he had so successfully worked out for his *Nudes in the Forest*. In *Three Figures* we find a simultaneous recurrence of the same "mechanized" personage: three figures taking shape in a complex of cones and cylinders, a serried mass of volumes traversed by broken rhythms, and a vortex of solid forms that, thanks to a skillful counterpoint of planes, gives rise to mysterious kaleidoscopic effects. Here the evocation of the rhythms of machinery in motion is far more precise than in *Nudes in the Forest*. The picture elements, on the other hand, are not adjusted to the same conceptual and chromatic unity. The homogeneity of the style of the *Nudes*—essentially nonrealist—was ensured by the clean-cut formal structure, whereas here the intermingling of realistic elements (the faces) with invented forms, and the insertion of illusionist motifs in non-illusionist space, leads to an ambivalence that is somewhat disconcerting. Moreover the color adds to this ambiguity; it undergoes a curious change of key around the sharply defined faces, then fans out in light, soft, tender tones. Later, Surrealism was to exploit this type of antinomy (quite other than the insertion of realistic details in an arrangement of colored facets which we find in Analytical Cubism). Yet, despite its shortcomings, *Three Figures* constitutes a bold attempt to render visual experience in an unorthodox manner and, as a product of imagination all compact, differs *toto caelo* from the works which the Cubists (Picasso and Braque) were then producing, chiefly in the form of still lifes. Léger's essentially dynamic art was poles apart from the static conceptions of Cubism. Cubism involved a breaking-up of volumes and staggered planes, whereas Léger's art was based

THE SMOKERS, 1911. COURTESY THE SOLOMON R. GUGGENHEIM MUSEUM, NEW YORK.

WOMAN IN BLUE, 1912. KUNSTMUSEUM, BASEL.

(anyhow provisionally) on the full rendering of volumes, on their echeloned arrangement, on their formal contrasts and movements in an heterogeneous space.

By and large, *Three Figures* was in the nature of an experiment, and derived less from any aesthetic theory than from the same moral and material, technical and social considerations as those which gave rise to Futurism. There is indeed a striking similarity between Marinetti's doctrines and the methods of Léger, the only vanguard French painter who, at this time, felt moved to celebrate the dynamism of modern life. It would seem that Léger painted the *Three Figures* in the period between the sensational appearance of the First Futurist Manifesto in the *Figaro* of February 20, 1909, and the publication of the Manifesto of Futurist Painting in *Comoedia*, May 18, 1910. "We wish at all costs," declared Balla, Boccioni, Carrà, Russolo and Severini in the second Manifesto, "to join forces with modern life. The triumphant science of today has abjured its past so as to answer better to the material requirements of our time... It is our hope that art, too, by discarding its past, will answer at long last to the intellectual requirements of the modern mind. Our growing need for Truth demands more than Forms and Colors treated on old-fashioned lines. What we seek to represent on canvas is no longer a momentary aspect of the universal dynamism but *the dynamic sensation itself*... Rejecting all the themes used in the past, we must express the trepidation of modern life, of our age of steel, of pride, of frenzied speed."[6]

The ideas enounced in the futurist program must have appealed to Léger and encouraged him to follow his natural bent.[7] However, the works actually produced by the Futurists, based as these were on the techniques of neo-impressionist Divisionism, were not to have any effect on his painting (in any case they were not on view in Paris until 1912). On the other hand, Delaunay, with whom he had entered into somewhat uneasy relations in 1909 and in whose company he had studied in 1910 Braque's and Picasso's "spider webs" at the Kahnweiler Gallery, had certainly something to do with the subtlety, elegance and musical effects we find in *The Wedding* (Musée d'Art Moderne, Paris). Here the broken lines, truncated forms, contrasts of black and white, and the "thorough-going mutation of the external and internal structure of the picture" owed much to Delaunay's experimental canvases, *The Town* (1910) and *The Windows* (also 1910).[8] Painted in 1911, immediately after *Three Figures*, *The Wedding* holds together better than its predecessor; the arbitrary conjunction of realistic and unrealistic elements is attenuated, the fragmentation of forms intensified, local color helps to define the "local scale" of volumes (still conic and cylindrical but more discreetly handled) and implements the chromatic values of occasional patches of flat color. The use of a bird's-eye perspective at once coordinates the lines of sight and gives an intriguingly elusive quality to the small nuclei of figurative elements disseminated on the picture surface.

These figurative allusions are less in evidence in the large *Woman in Blue* (1912), whose radiance illuminates the whole wall on which it hangs at the Kunstmuseum, Basel. Noteworthy in this fully thought-out work is the artist's masterly handling of elision and the superb transfiguration of a familiar motif: a stately matron in an armchair, seen in front view.[9] Here two elements of Léger's compositional technique—dark outlines binding forms and tracts of absolutely flat color—make their appearance. Another novelty is the conflict between linearism and expression by volumes, and planes are emphasized by the employment of pure color. An unbalance ingeniously compensated for by the use of geometric forms (rectangles, trapezia, circles, triangles), and an asymmetrical interplay of solids (cones, cylinders) play their part in the masterly orchestration of this well-planned work.

LANDSCAPE, 1911. KUNSTHISTORISCHES MUSEUM, VIENNA.

AN AESTHETIC OF CONTRASTS

The Mobility of Color

> It seems to me that the creative act is determined
> less by the gaps left in past achievements than
> by the fullness of a new life that has not yet
> found expression; a superabundance over-
> riding what preceded it, and showing up its
> inadequacy.
>
> GAËTAN PICON

IN 1909 Léger mistrusted color; he admitted that he "hadn't yet learnt how to make it 'tell.' " With Delaunay's help he lit on an original solution of his problem. "I wanted," he told André Verdet, "to get at tones that can stand by themselves, a very red red, a very blue blue. Delaunay went in for nuances, I for forthright colors... In 1912 I started using pure colors enclosed in geometric forms—e.g. the *Woman in Blue*."[10]

This was a decisive forward step, and it proved that he was now determined to shake off Cézanne's influence. "He had such a hold of me," Léger said, "that I had to go all abstract to escape. In *Woman in Blue* I felt that at last I'd got Cézanne out of my system and by the same token traveled far from the impressionist *bel canto*."[11]

Viewed in its historical context, this canvas strikes us as the most brilliant and most thorough-going of all the attempts made in the venturesome years immediately preceding the First World War to interpret reality in non-figurative terms. Nor need we be surprised if in October of that year, 1912, the *Woman in Blue* was one of the most violently attacked pictures shown at the Salon d'Automne. The doyen of the Paris Town

Council addressed an open letter to the then Minister of Fine Arts which reflected the prevailing feelings on the subject. "If the voice of a Town Councillor can make itself heard in your Ministry, I would beg you, sir, to cast a glance at this year's Salon d'Automne. Only go there and, I hope, you will leave this exhibition feeling no less disgusted than are many people whom I know. I venture to hope that you will ask yourself *sotto voce*, 'Have I really the right to lend a public edifice to a gang of miscreants who are behaving in the world of art exactly like the apaches who infest certain streets of Paris?' Leaving that exhibition, you well may wonder if nature and the human form have ever before been vilified so grossly, and you will be forced to recognize that this Salon is a hotbed of every imaginable type of ugliness and vulgarity."[12]

The chief formal innovation of *Woman in Blue*—the use of flat tracts of pure, unbroken color bound with tight-drawn lines—was not followed up by the artist in the immediate future, except in *Nude Model in the Studio* (1912, Solomon R. Guggenheim Museum, New York), which seems to combine two parallel lines of research. For Léger had not shaken off as completely as he claimed the influences of Impressionism and Cézanne. During this period he produced a group of pictures—*Landscape* (1911, Kunsthistorisches Museum, Vienna), *The Smokers* (1911, Solomon R. Guggenheim Museum, New York), *Level Crossing* (1912) and *The Roofs of Paris* (1912), both in the Musée Fernand Léger, Biot—which keep closer to the facts of visual experience. In these works Cézannesque Cubism, of the years 1907-1908, is associated with the more direct approach of the Fauves and, in particular, of Delaunay (in *The Eiffel Tower*, 1910). We are reminded of Aragon's lines:

Le paysage s'est pris les collines dans un filet de baraquements,
Le paysage a mis des colliers de fumées.

LEVEL CROSSING, 1912. MUSÉE FERNAND LÉGER, BIOT.

In these scenes of the heart of the city, of the outskirts of a village, or of suburban life, forms are "modulated" in light, in a sheen of pale, misty colors, on a field of fleecy undulations and geometric rhythms. Signposts mark out space, as Uccello's lances punctuated it in a former age. Caught up in the speed dimension and glimpsed apparently in a split second as an express hurtles by, roofs come cataracting down, level-crossing gates swing out, poles flash up through spherical leafage and dappled skies. Cézanne aspired to paint "the moment of the world"; Léger gives us "the world of the moment." A sense of speed is fused into the color sense. Next, after mastering the plane of pure color and winning as he said "the battle of volumes," our painter, like Delaunay, tested out the possibilities of nuances. That he now was trying to render atmosphere is evident. Now, too, for the first time he tackled systematically the problem of suggesting depth and, starting out from the classical method (whose allusive power he modified), he spaced out planes oriented in several directions, broke up the erstwhile unity of the cube viewed in perspective and with it the evident weight of real things and their strictly sensorial attributes. Here, again, but only tentatively, he joined forces with Delaunay, who was trying to devise "an arrangement of colors evoking at once static values and movement."[13]

For Léger these were exceptionally productive years and by the age of thirty he had become one of the best known figures of the Left Bank. He took part in all the avant-garde exhibitions, and his work was shown at Barcelona, Brussels and Moscow. His career was followed with keen interest by Max Jacob, Maurice Raynal, Gertrude Stein, Pierre Reverdy and Walter Pach. "I enjoy his work," Apollinaire remarked, "because he's never high-brow, never lowers himself and never argufies," and he appreciated the man himself as much for his simplicity as for his "sound good sense."[14] Like Marcel Duchamp,

La Fresnaye, Picabia, Gleizes, Metzinger and Kupka, he was a member of the Puteaux Group which met regularly at Jacques Villon's studio. On Sundays he often paid a visit, with Delaunay, to the worthy Douanier, whose "frank and downright way of painting" he admired, and it was Rousseau who led him to discover and appreciate the static, majestically compelling art of Louis David. An habitué of the Rotonde, the café which the Montparnassian avant-garde was to render famous, he acted now and then as bodyguard to Modigliani when he insisted on treating the company to a song despite the protests of the proprietor of the café. Léger's resonant voice, his pungent wit and trenchant aphorisms were much appreciated at the dinners of the "Passy artists," and he often went to the weekly soirées at Canudo's office. "There one met Rodin, Loie Fuller, all the celebrities of the period, but also the new men. Fernand Léger, taciturn and rather intimidating he looked like an English boxer—used to stay put in a corner, thinking dark thoughts. At bottom Léger always despised society gatherings."[15]

He rarely visited art galleries, and enjoyed the Salon de l'Aviation far more than the Louvre. He went there once with Marcel Duchamp and Brancusi, his favorite sculptor. "Marcel, a silent sort of chap—you never knew what he was thinking—inspected the engines and propellers without saying a word. Then suddenly he remarked to Brancusi, 'It's all up with painting. What painter could improve on that propeller? Could you, could any of us make anything as good?' He adored *real* things, so did we all, but not so fanatically as he... Personally," Léger adds, "I was more attracted by the engines and metallic parts than by the wooden propellers."[16]

He now was backed by the picture dealer D. H. Kahnweiler, then a young man, who in the autumn of 1912 organized Léger's first one-man show, a token of confidence highly welcome to the artist at the time. The following year (on October 20, 1913)

WOMAN IN AN ARMCHAIR, 1912.
COLLECTION OF MR AND MRS HARRY LEWIS WINSTON, BIRMINGHAM, MICH.

WOMAN IN RED AND GREEN, 1914.
MUSÉE NATIONAL D'ART MODERNE, PARIS.

Kahnweiler, who had just taken Braque, Picasso and Derain under his wing, drew up a contract giving him exclusive rights in Léger's output—a godsend to the artist, who was now relieved from the daily struggle to make ends meet.[17]

This too was the time when, feeling surer of himself and rid of his "provincial" shyness, Léger made bold to air his views in print. He contributed to the first issue of *Montjoie*, oddly described as the "organ of French artistic imperialism," and articles by him also appeared in the Berlin periodical, *Der Sturm*. On May 5, 1913, he delivered (at the Académie Wassilieff) his first lecture. In this, when describing the origins of contemporary painting—the subject of the address—he stated *inter alia* that "many people have an idea that modern painting will revert to what is commonly regarded as 'ordinary' painting. This idea is quite unfounded. When an art such as this new art is in full possession of its means and these enable it to bring off works that are completely self-sufficient, it is bound to hold its own over a very long time. I am convinced that the conception of art we are now arriving at measures up to the scope and standards of the greatest periods of the past."[18]

His rising prestige, the feeling that young though he was his views were taken seriously, emboldened him, and the years 1912-1913 marked the beginning of a brilliantly experimental phase. His vision suddenly acquired a new amplitude and his pictorial architecture dimensions in the grand style. Shaking off the influence of Delaunay and taking Cézanne's art as his point of departure, Léger embarked on a highly personal and original type of Fauvism, and exploited to brilliant effect a formal structure based on the dissociation of line and color.

In a magnificent sequence of "Variations of Forms"— *Woman in an Armchair* (1912, Winston Collection, Birmingham, Mich.), *The Staircase* (1913, Kunsthaus, Zurich), *Contrasts of Forms* (1913, Philadelphia Museum of Art), *The Lamp* (1913,

Block Collection, Chicago), *Contrasts of Forms* (1913, Rupf Collection, Bern), *Woman in Red and Green* (1914, Musée d'Art Moderne, Paris), and other works of this period—pure color, released from the cage of outlines, runs free and sings, weaving its way among contrasts of forms that state the key themes of the movement. Vibrant through and through, changing only very slightly when it rounds a curve or glides across a flat expanse, this color always suggests, never describes. Léger's color seems to have a life of its own, devouring all it comes in contact with, and though its range is limited to red, blue and yellow, these are activated by a play of contrasts skillfully enhanced by passages of white (the raw white of the canvas).

In the result the picture, whatever its source of inspiration, still life or human life, might be described as auto-figurative; it speaks for itself in its own language. Objects seem made of ductile metal—of pieces of folded, soldered, hammered-out sheet-iron that interlock—and yet are strangely dematerialized. Once again we have a maze of expansible surfaces, cones and cylinders, but here they are traversed by glancing lights and transfigured by the vibrant line which allots them their appropriate places under an abstract illumination. The eye is fascinated by these dancing forms, forever regrouping themselves in a rhythmic continuum, a counterpoint of contrasts. As a result of these planned contrasts, between circular and angular, two- and three-dimensional forms, color (the three basic primary colors) develops a remarkable mobility. And in such canvases as *The Houses under the Trees* (1913, Folkwang Museum, Essen) or *Village in the Forest* (1914, Kunstmuseum, Basel), it is yet again the painter himself "who seems born out of these things, as if by dint of concentration and an influx of the visible" (Merleau-Ponty). One has an impression that everything is in motion in an indeterminate space; walls and roofs are treated like stage sets, tree trunks like the rotating shafts of a turbine.

HOUSES UNDER THE TREES, 1913. FOLKWANG MUSEUM, ESSEN.

VILLAGE IN THE FOREST, 1914. KUNSTMUSEUM, BASEL.

THE STAIRCASE, 1913. KUNSTHAUS, ZURICH.

Let us now imagine the linear structure of these pictures tightened up, the forms hardening and organized in a stricter figurative cohesion, and the colors put to the service of plasticity—then perhaps we can understand how the artist came to paint in 1917 that large and justly famous work *The Card Party* (Kröller-Müller Museum, Otterlo).

In 1914, a few months before the war, Léger had delivered a second lecture at the Académie Wassilieff, in which he expounded the new trends of his art. "If the whole way of painting has changed, it's because modern life has made this necessary. The creative artist's existence nowadays is far more condensed, more complicated than it was in the past. The thing depicted is less stable, even the object-in-itself less discernible than it used to be. Landscapes you cross in an express train or a car lose in descriptive value but gain in synthetic value; the window of the railroad carriage or the driving mirror of your car, combined with the speed you're traveling at, have changed the normal look of things. Modern man registers a hundred times more impressions than those of eighteenth-century man—this is reflected even in our present-day speech, full of diminutives and abbreviations. The condensation of the modern picture, its diversity, its dislocated forms—all result from the tempo of modern life."[10]

THREE COMRADES, 1920. STEDELIJK MUSEUM, AMSTERDAM.

BALLET MECANIQUE

Undertones of War

It is in relation to a man's whole life that an
object can be beautiful.

GILBERT SIMONDON

THE declaration of war found Delaunay in Spain and Le
Fauconnier in Holland. Braque was at Sorgues when he got
his marching orders; Picasso (who had spent the summer working with Derain in Provence) saw Braque off on the platform
of Avignon station. A far-ranging venture of the mind came
to an end with brutal suddenness, and the groups of vanguard
artists were dispersed. Apollinaire, Zadkine, Marcoussis volun-
teered for service in the French army. La Fresnaye, though
invalided out by a medical board, enlisted. Villon, Gleizes,
Duchamp Villon and others were mobilized. Léger, too, on
August 2, 1914, was called up for service.

For him the war provided a unique experience, at once psychological, visual and emotive, of the miseries and grandeur of
the human situation. It did not deflect him from his path; on the
contrary, the rigors of army life in wartime made him even surer
of his vocation and, in facing up to the ordeal, he developed a
wonderful peace of mind. Those "four years without colors"
opened his eyes to the possibilities of comradeship, the true
significance of peace, the demands of freedom, and reinforced
his sense of commitment to his art.

55

MAN WITH A PIPE, 1916. PHILIPPE DOTREMONT COLLECTION, UCCLE (BRUSSELS).

"It was at the front," he told his friend Pierre Descargues, "that I learned everything, understood everything, and found the true *raison d'être* of my painting. Try to imagine all that this abrupt immersion in the war could mean to me. Giving up my work in the studio, my 'abstract' experimentation, I was plunged into the company of men for whom the question 'life or death?' no longer counted and who from the first day of the war knew they were doomed men living on reprieve."[20]

"My war experience," he said on another occasion, "acted as a revelation or, if you will, an illumination. Suddenly I found myself rubbing shoulders with the entire French people; my new companions were miners, navvies, workers in wood or metal... And I was struck by the fine qualities, the sense of humor, the *perfection* of many of the men around me, their quickness to perceive what was of practical use and the best way of turning it to account, in the midst of the daily life-and-death struggle in which we were helplessly involved. Some of these men were poets of a kind, inventors of truly poetic, if homely, turns of speech—I have in mind the colorful, changeful *argot* of the trenches."[21] Léger decided that henceforth his paintings were to be as forthright as this *argot*, "pointed, terse, robust."

He was well equipped for this; thanks to his peasant background, he felt at home among his fellow soldiers, could mix with them on equal terms, speak their language, forthright to the point of crudity, and reflect this easy intercourse in his art. This "animal matter teeming with vitality" incited him to a complete surrender to an obscure force within, a return to the sources of his creative impulse. And when these "marvelous fellows, frank and sturdy as trees" (their nickname for him was "Ginger"), played cards in their billets behind the lines, he watched them with an artist's eye and took their measure. He never tired of drawing them, exactly as they were. The idea of this came to him spontaneously, he said. But equally spontaneously he worked into depictions of them the forms of guns, shell-cases, breech-blocks, field kitchens—all the familiar, exciting things that daily met his eye.[22]

Preliminary to the *Man with a Pipe* (Dotremont Collection, Brussels, formerly Rolf de Maré Collection, Stockholm) was the figurative drawing, *Soldier* (1914, Douglas Cooper Collection, France); next came an experimental variant, *The Smoker* (1916, Madame Frigerio Collection, Paris). The final version, painted in 1916 when Léger was on leave in Paris, is at once a condensation, a gesture of defiance and a dramatic synthesis, in which a single note of vermilion tells shrilly out in a mass of cold, rigid, dull-hued forms. This provocative work points the way to the famous *Card Party* in the Kröller-Müller Museum, Otterlo. (Three preliminary sketches exist: 1915, Lord Amulree Collection, London; 1916, Douglas Cooper Collection, France; 1916, Musée Fernand Léger, Biot.) On the back of the canvas is an inscription: *Made in Paris on sick leave, December 1917.* The subject is a compact group of privates and NCOs, some wearing helmets, some kepis, all smoking pipes. The idea of this picture had gradually taken form during the long months he spent in hospital after being gassed on the Verdun front in September 1916. In these card players, these *poilus* morally and physically mechanized, depersonalized and reduced to the state of semi-human robots—the common lot of the private soldier in the Great War—we have in fact a new version of *Nudes in the Forest*. But here the figures have so to say matured, as a result of the ordeal the artist has lived through. Denizens of a closed world based on the flawless unity of the circle, and stemming from the inhuman arsenal of the war machine, they have taken on the geometrical shapes of breech-blocks, the volumes of high explosive shells, the sheen of steel.

Admirably composed, this work associates the bright colors (blue, red, yellow) of *Variations of Forms* with the arbitrary physical structure of the woodcutters, and flat color with modulated volumes, in a complex of pseudo-shadows and unreal light. In point of fact, this was not the first time Léger deliberately chose a strictly contemporary subject and there is no doubt that these new stylistic developments were favored by the events in which he was now involved. But another factor of capital importance contributed to the plastic plenitude and originality of this work, and this was Léger's "discovery" of the motion picture, in whose techniques he found much in common with the program he had set himself in his painting.

On short leave in 1916, when he was painting the *Man with a Pipe*, Léger was taken by Apollinaire to a Montparnasse picture house where they were showing an early Chaplin film. "So I saw the great Charlie Chaplin," he subsequently told a friend, "and I'll say this for his performance, that it held its own quite well beside the 'big show' I'd just quitted at the front. This funny little man, who succeeds in being not only a funny little man, but also a sort of living puppet, dry as a stick, with clickety joints—this was something new!" True, this was something new—but the same might be said of Léger's *poilu*, treated like a puppet with exactly the same jerky movements, the same clockwork-like gestures as those of the great little comedian, and actuated by the same rhythm as the first (silent) films. No less new were the dimensions of the card players in the foreground, who definitely remind us of one of the most striking effects of the early movies: the "close up" projected from the screen into the spectator's space.

In January 1918, at the end of his convalescent leave, Léger, whose health had been seriously impaired, was invalided out of the army. That he was fit enough, however, to paint, was demonstrated by *The Card Party*, in which the painter's total mastery of his medium is plain to see. A consummation of tendencies implicit in the earlier works, it is animated with that "perpetual inner movement" which was one of Léger's personal discoveries. Here his aim is once again to suggest a relationship between man and the machine and, far from inaugurating (as some have said) a new phase, it is rather a summing up of his intentions, a signpost on the path he had mapped out. Henceforth his artistic evolution at once speeds up and gains in depth. Taking his stand, as he said, at the antipodes of Impressionism, he gives ever freer rein to his completely personal vision.

"We employ our senses," Léger once remarked, "more than ever before; we use our eyes, ears, hands and feet to see, hear, and touch a multitude of things. We try to see clearly, to understand machinery, the functioning of motor engines down to the least detail... The age I live in surrounds me with manufactured objects, perfect of their kind and for their purpose." Some rusty, battered old lamps, "found where the scavengers dump their rubbish," had once (in 1885) roused Van Gogh's enthusiasm. And today Dubuffet finds in "dirty floors and bits of dusty ground" sources of "glamour and delight."[23] It was Léger who discovered the *beauty* of a dynamo, a printing press, ball bearings, gear levers. "The idea of a graded, classified, docketed beauty is fallacious. Beauty is everywhere: in the arrangement of your pots and pans on the white kitchen wall, more so perhaps than in your eighteenth-century furniture or in the official museums. Once you grant this point, you will agree with me about the beauty of machinery."[24] These observations (and many others) show how Léger's entire œuvre is the outcome of a new mode of sensibility, one that is no longer stimulated by a violin, a naked woman or a tobacco jar, but by the machine-made objects that he boldly converts first into aesthetic realities, then into poetic symbols.

It is obvious that Léger's way of seeing was the direct consequence of radical changes in the contemporary conception of the world of forms, and of the relations between the seeing

THE CARD PARTY, 1917.
RIJKSMUSEUM KRÖLLER-MÜLLER, OTTERLO (HOLLAND).

eye and actuality. He saw, felt and thought in terms of the
technical developments which were giving its new, distinctive
look to an age characterized above all by the persistent, ever
more widespread incursion of machinery into daily life. That
mechanical contrivances—cylinders, propellers, disks, gear
wheels, couplings and the like—were his main source of inspiration from 1918 to 1920, was due undoubtedly to his wish to
detect in machinery "human gestures embodied and crystallized
in structures that *work*."[25] For he was fully aware that the

THE PROPELLERS, 1918. COLLECTION, THE MUSEUM OF MODERN ART, NEW YORK.
KATHERINE S. DREIER BEQUEST.

Lég. 22

ACROBATS IN THE CIRCUS, 1918.
KUNSTMUSEUM, BASEL.

machine was imparting a new *quality* to civilization. The chief concern, and indeed the true originality of Léger's art, lay in his attempt to understand that quality, and this implied the personal philosophy which was "the guiding principle of his life."[26]

Should we regard this as "a naïve and credulous" philosophy, did Léger make a fetish of *homo faber*, and did he deliberately

THE DISKS, 1918. MUSÉE D'ART MODERNE DE LA VILLE DE PARIS.

"harness his creative activity to scientific and industrial norms?"[27] Surely it is truer to say that the serene perceptiveness he brought to bear when "facing up to the world of the machine" implied an active participation in what was a living reality of the age and a willing acceptance of its major values. Others no doubt regarded that world with somewhat jaundiced eyes and, bent chiefly on "expressing themselves," chose the solution of escapism. The machine age jarred on them and they vented their resentment by decrying the machine and all its works. Those "angry young men" the Dadaists doubtless served as catalysers in their obstreperous heyday. But Dadaism ended up with "kicking aside the work of art, that ball-and-chain which holds the soul down after death."[28] *Au fond* the Dadaists were afraid of the machine; subconsciously they sensed in it a peril. Thus, paradoxically enough, those nihilistic non-conformists who set out to shock the bourgeois and to shatter all conventional ideas of art and morality, adopted what is the commonest, most typical attitude of the middle-class mind, which saw (and still sees) in the machine and technical appliances "robots animated with hostile intentions *(sic)* towards Man, and always liable to turn against their maker and eliminate him."[29]

This only goes to show "how thoroughly unbalanced is our present-day culture, up in arms against technology and all its works." That antagonism between culture and technique, art and science, man and the machine, of which we hear so much today tends (as Gilbert Simondon justly observes in a brilliant study of the subject) "to mask behind a specious humanism a reality rich in human achievement," and also, we would add, of deep significance for modern man. It was this reality that Léger perceived and faithfully revealed, and in this respect his œuvre acted as a bridge between the two worlds. Léger's art affected people in different ways. In some cases it undermined the romantic notion that the machines and machine-made objects which meet our eyes at every turn are aesthetically null, without any possible appeal to the cultured sensibility. Others, however, came to understand that such objects can have emotive values of their own and were fortified in the belief that the technical achievements of the modern world are entitled to an honored place in the domain of culture.

Outstanding creations of this decisive period are three epoch-making works. First we have the superb *Acrobats in the Circus* (1918, Kunstmuseum, Basel; initial version, 1918, Dutilleul Collection, Paris; third state, 1920, Paul Rosenberg Gallery, New York), whose morphology derives directly from the *Card Party*. Next, that audacious synthesis, *The City* (1919-1920, Philadelphia Museum of Art), and finally *The Disks* (1918, Musée d'Art Moderne de la Ville de Paris), with its compelling symbolism. Thus transposed into painting, the technical data acquire a total unreality, and to describe this art as "fundamentally mechanical," as some have done, is as unjust as it is inept. For it involves an appraisal of the work in terms of what it *seems* to represent and a failure to perceive the new poetic vision which went to its making. Here the artist's celebration of the machine age is creative through and through; so much so that he invents forms and colors which, as Maurice Blanchot suggests, attract our gaze to them and divert it from the raw material of reality. "The painter never proceeds from the visible world to art but always from art towards forms that have the look of *neutralized* appearances of the world."[30]

This is why it would be equally wrong to regard the work of art as a testimony and the painter as a "witness to his age." Like Aragon's novels, Léger's pictures are *emanations* of the age he lived in; it was in terms of the Zeitgeist that he built up a world whose paintable elements were governed by an inner logic, a logic independent of their purely technical applications. "I invent pictures of machines," Léger once said, "as others

66

MECHANICAL ELEMENTS, 1918-1923. KUNSTMUSEUM, BASEL.

conjure up landscapes in their imagination." "This, it seems, accounts for his habit of scanning objects of the workaday world from a special angle, of neutralizing their normal functions, of purifying them, and elevating them by progressive stylizations to a momentary equilibrium in which they become the stuff of painting."[31] Thus the disk, that homely signal of our streets and railroads, becomes a specifically pictorial element, a keyword in a syntax of forms. Diverted from its practical uses, it acts as "a point of transit for the lifeline of the picture"—in short, the signal becomes a sign, standing for the entire mechanistic universe. In the last analysis, *The Disks* symbolizes the geometric order which environs modern man. These disks function in an imaginary space, where volumes are non-existent, and pure, vivid colors are rendered in flat tones, with here and there triangular formations cutting through the local hues of the concentric circles. Quite reasonably we may see in this a protest against the purposive disruption practised by the Cubists; also a riposte to the circular forms, based on optical sensations, which Delaunay was then employing.

The City, too, starts out from a theme employed, in 1910, by Delaunay but, needless to say, handled by him quite differently. In this masterly composition, the fruit of long research, and a symbolic figuration of a twentieth-century city, Léger skillfully leads our gaze away from the purely structural elements—a poster, a stencilled letter, a pylon, a metal staircase, etc.—and directs it to forms existing in their own right without regard to their utilitarian functions. Here the roughly indicated letter (Braque had introduced the letter into painting in 1911) stresses the contrast between the literal reality it *is* and the abstract reality it stands for. White plays an exceptionally active part, intercalated between zones of vivid reds, yellows, greens, blues and pungent black. Though this work clearly owes much to Synthetic Cubism, the way that form and color are combined

THE TYPOGRAPHER, 1919. RIJKSMUSEUM KRÖLLER-MÜLLER, OTTERLO (HOLLAND).

70

THE CITY, 1919-1920. A.E. GALLATIN COLLECTION,
PHILADELPHIA MUSEUM OF ART.

strikes a quite new note. Without recourse to chiaroscuro, modulation or staggered planes, Léger suggests depth simply by assigning a spatial value—more pronounced than in his previous works—to flat tracts of color. Moreover he manipulates inert, static, sharply defined and disconnected forms in such a way as to create an overall dynamic tension. Finally, the liberation of color is now complete and it is treated as an independent entity. It is interesting to note that this concept of the autonomy of color was, in the same period, basic to the Dutch Neo-Plasticism.

Into this all-inclusive system Léger was bound to reintroduce the human figure. To begin with he painted it in direct contact with machinery. The brilliantly conceived *Typographer* (1919, sketch, Kröller-Müller Museum, Otterlo; first state, 1918, Private Collection, New York; second state, Carré Gallery, Paris) combines frankly mimetic elements with an inner logic, in a plastically and rationally coherent structure. To the following year dates *The Woman with a Mirror* (1920, National Museum, Stockholm), in which the looking glass reflects with ruthless accuracy the ordered disorder of tectonic forms to which even the figure automatically adjusts itself; here more than ever "the image assumes the form of its substructure."

ABSTRACT COMPOSITION, 1919. MUSÉE FERNAND LÉGER, BIOT.

A STATIC COMPENSATION

The Lure of the Wall

> One invents a technique or procedure by one-
> self; one does not invent entirely on one's own
> *a state of mind.*
>
> JUAN GRIS

M AN painted before he built, and he has never ceased to bear
in mind the priority of that first creative gesture. Always
the painter has given the lead to the builder, and in the light
of this indubitable fact the problem of the relations between
painting and architecture needs to be restated and thought out
afresh. Once this is done their seeming rivalry is seen to be
a myth, the old idea of architecture as the Mother of the Arts
collapses, and certain modern pretensions to "a synthesis of the
arts" (as in the Unesco Building in Paris) prove to be both specious and sterile, since any real fusion of different modes of
plastic expression has to be secret and spontaneous, a natural
product of the historical context.

Painting may be defined as, basically, a manifestation of the
relations between man and the world around him. These vary
according to the age and place in which they take their rise.
We believe that a close study of these relations (which obviously
lies outside the scope of this monograph) would show that
from the earliest times painting has stolen a march on architecture—in the sense of prefiguring developments that subsequently
took place in the architectural domain—and also that, thanks to

his creative imagination, the artist has visualized the spatial settings which sooner or later man elects for his dwelling places, scenes of his activities or leisure, or places of repose and meditation. In other words painting under one of its aspects (that of a cultural or social factor) can often be regarded as an experimental means of interpreting visual, spatial, linear and formal concepts to which subsequently architecture attempts to give material form, though not always with success (Piranesi's poetic visions of imaginary edifices had no perceptible effect on everyday reality). It should be possible—and highly interesting—to trace the many ways in which the discoveries and inventions of painters have found fulfillment in architecture, and to show how much the Mother of the Arts has owed to the primordial inspiration of her "daughter."

This is why—to take a modern instance—we cannot endorse the view recently expressed [32] that there is an "unbridgeable gulf" between Mies van der Rohe and Jackson Pollock. Indeed any such gulf is unthinkable, for the good reason that Van der Rohe's architecture is a direct outcome of the immediate past, an exact realization of theories already advanced in *De Stijl* and at the Bauhaus. The paintings of Jackson Pollock, Sam Francis and Mark Rothko, on the other hand, have still to await the as yet undreamt-of architecture that will body forth their concepts. When Mondrian observed that "so long as a wholly new architecture has not come into being, it is up to painting to do what architecture has so far failed to do," he sensed instinctively that intimate relationship between the two arts which we have here in mind—a relationship that (without, however, grasping its profounder implications) he was to fructify deliberately in a series of remarkable creations.

A derivative of Cubism, Neo-Plasticism set out to do away with the representational elements still existing in that movement and totally to modify pictorial structure by concentrating

MECHANICAL ELEMENTS ON A RED GROUND, 1924.
MUSÉE FERNAND LÉGER, BIOT.

on linear framework, rectangular planes, dynamic contrasts, "open" forms, peripheric development, the exclusion of curves, a carefully restricted palette. What concerns us here is less the communicative value of this austere art (which in fact might have led to purely negative results) than its basic principles: strict coherence, constructive logic and a formal spareness so satisfying to the eye that its repercussions on three-dimensional space were almost immediate and its sphere of influence surprisingly wide (covering the whole of Europe). The so-called "cubist" architecture (here the epithet is literally applicable) of the 1920s exploited in steel, glass and concrete the spatial methods of Neo-Plasticism, stripped surfaces of non-essentials, clarified volumes, invited the play of light and added color. Thus the whole conception of architectural design was modified; the edifice was treated as an open field for the dynamic interplay of horizontal planes (predominant), vertical planes (relatively short) and transparent planes (an innovation).

Though Mondrian and Van Doesburg foresaw the architectural applications of their art and made no secret of this, Léger had no inkling of the future of his own discoveries. At most he had a vague idea of the general relevance of contemporary painting to the architecture of the time which, as he remarked, "by the force of things evolves more slowly and tends to lag behind the spirit of the age."[33] On the face of it, no doubt, his lifelong interest in architecture may be accounted for by his early training. But it struck deeper than that. When round about 1920 he experienced what might be described as "the lure of the wall"—felt drawn, that is to say, to mural art—this was due to several causes: to an intuitive understanding of the psychic and physical functions of color ("pure color's a stunning raw material, as indispensable to life as fire and water"); also to a sense of social justice ("colored space is for the poor a vital need"); and finally to a sharp reaction against four years of drabness

Lég. 29

MURAL COMPOSITION, 1924. MUSÉE FERNAND LÉGER, BIOT.

Lég. 30

COMPOSITION, 1925.
COURTESY THE SOLOMON R. GUGGENHEIM MUSEUM, NEW YORK.

("No sooner was the war over than color came into its own and soon it bulked large in daily life. My instinctive desire for colors was promptly seconded by the street, by the city."[34]).

When engaged on that vast work *The City*, Léger suddenly felt cramped by the dimensions of the easel picture. He was conscious of a physical need to enlarge his field of action, to give himself more elbow room. After successfully assimilating (again in *The City*) the lessons of Synthetic Cubism, he decided to carry these a stage further by developing the possibilities of flat tones and endowing color with complete autonomy. This, naturally enough, led him to perceive a vocation hitherto but dimly apprehended in the midst of other preoccupations: his aptitude for mural painting. (The reader must not take this to mean that we endorse the all too prevalent notion of mural painting as being necessarily two-dimensional, since the illusion of a third dimension at any point would impair the wall's integrity. The hotly debated problem of "hollowing out" or not "hollowing out" the wall is quite irrelevant. The great thing is so to arrange the composition as at once to bring out volume and to magnify the value of a given space. Contemporary painting is no more specifically mural in intent than was Michelangelo's. Here, too, we must take care not to lump together two quite different problems: the problem of mural painting is basically technical and concerns a fusion of styles; on the other hand, the "architectural" potentialities of painting—a more exacting problem—are conditioned by a functional prototype.)

In this phase Léger was all the more convinced of the bi-dimensionality of the wall surface because he saw in it a palliative for his overwrought sensibility, the constant strain imposed on his imagination by the program he had set himself. The *De Stijl* publications circulated in Paris from 1920 on by the Galerie de L'Effort Moderne—with which, at Léonce Rosenberg's invitation, he was associated for three years, before migrating to

Kahnweiler's "boutique cubiste"—endorsed his then distaste for figuration and confirmed his belief in the "denaturalization" which, on his own initiative, he had practised in 1919 (*The City*). He was much encouraged by Mondrian and Van Doesburg when he met them in 1921. He had never brought himself to ostracize the curve, but these champions of "pure" painting now incited him to an exclusive (if short-lived) use of right angles. Delighted by their stand against "traditions, dogmas and the prerogatives of individualism," he saw in Neo-Plasticism "a total liberation, a crying need, a means of getting certain poisons out of our system." Also, no doubt, he welcomed it as an antidote to the ironic negativism of the Dadaists, and as an optimistic product of the war "which had made an end of the world of yesterday and all its ideas" (First De Stijl Manifesto, 1918). Neo-Plasticism's aversion for symmetry appealed to him (symmetry, he said, was "a dead letter"), as did its penchant for geometry ("the man of today lives in a preponderantly geometrical environment").

Léger now embarked on a series of strictly abstract works, made with an eye to architectural adaptations (*Mural Compositions*, 1924, Fernand Léger Museum, Biot; 1924, Nelson Rockefeller Collection, New York; 1924-1925, Madame Y. Zervos Collection, Paris; 1929, Private Collection, Geneva, etc.). This was a rewarding experience, involving as it did "a skillful, grandiose presentment of colored forces in motion on the surface of the wall."[35] "Here Léger," as Le Corbusier noted, "went beyond the turbulent diagonals of machinery; the turbulence was now no longer in the drawing but derived from the movement of the colors, advancing or receding. This was the dynamic factor in his composition."[36] Only a step was needed to dispense with composition altogether and to exploit within an architectural frame of reference the specific qualities of color. "The apartment, which I may define as a 'habitable rectangle,' will be transformed into an 'elastic rectangle.' A light blue wall recedes, a black one comes forward, and a yellow one disappears. One can ring the changes on them *ad infinitum*."[37]

For all its rationality this notion has its dangers, since it may well upset all the relations envisaged by the architect and play havoc with the basic qualities of a given space. On occasion, however, it may serve to palliate a lack of architectural amenities. "It is in the humble dwellings where workers have to live, that the need for color is most strongly felt," as Léger rightly said. "They must be given space, and no serious attempt has yet been made to provide this. The poor man, the poor family cannot afford the fine work of art that, hung on the wall, would give a sense of spatial freedom. For such families colored space is a vital need. It's up to us to fill the room with color-light."[38]

It is clear, nonetheless, that Léger's true contribution to contemporary art lay in the new, strange world of forms in which he gave free play to his creative inspiration: a world essentially dynamic and rich in intimations. That architect of vision Le Corbusier was fully alive to the possibilities opened up by Léger's painting. "Of all the painters practising today," he said (in 1929), "Léger is the one whose pictures call most imperatively for a new architecture... In this he differs from all our contemporary masters whose pictures, by the very law of their being, can forgather with the architecture of the past. That of course is why his works so greatly scandalize the public."[39]

STILL LIFE WITH AN ARM, 1927. FOLKWANG MUSEUM, ESSEN.

A DIALECTIC OF CONTRARIES

Objects in Space

Your right arm is the arm of the lyre, and your left that of the compass. With it you can regale yourself with stars at every meal.

BOURDELLE

Léger believed he had found in abstract painting a means —the ideal means—of bringing color into the grey heart of the city: color that was a "song without words" directly appealing to the man in the street. At the 1925 Exhibition of Decorative Arts Le Corbusier and Mallet-Stevens gave him an opportunity of testing out his theories. We would, however, be wrong to regard this as constituting an isolated or distinctive episode in his artistic evolution.

For the critic's or art historian's convenience—or with a view to tracing more clearly the development of a style a habit has arisen of dividing up an artist's œuvre into successive "periods," distinguishable by the predominance of certain subjects. Nothing could be more misleading, more inept. Here we have yet another instance of what might be described as an atomistic psychology; of that old-fashioned analytic method which thrives on arbitrary dislocations and neatly segregated patterns. But this method, tending as it does to disrupt the basic unity of an artist's output, drains it of all vitality. For the body of work an artist gives the world forms an organic whole, with all its parts interlocking, overlapping, interpenetrating and

83

reciprocally enriched and energized throughout an entire career by their own past, present and future manifestations.

In the case of Léger's art, the abstract components can be understood only in the light of the painter's oeuvre as a whole. Viewed in this context, the fact that they were the inevitable corollary of a program to which he adhered at every stage of his life, and which is exemplified in *The City*, becomes apparent. For then we see that the abstract elements are essentially *concomitant* with frankly figurative details, and that the artist's recourse to them did not involve any weakening or abeyance of his innate passion for the real. When Léger ventured into abstractionism he did not withdraw himself from the world of visual experience, tactile values, sensuous responses, nor did this new interest alienate him from those "natural forces" with which he had proclaimed his total solidarity. Rather, he brought it into line with his other aspirations. On a compositional schema (of "open," peripheral forms) deriving from it, the rectangular plane is treated as a ground for the curves and volumes of partial or complete objects, and these objects are always massive, sculpturesque and "closed." And in *Still Life with an Arm* (1927, Folkwang Museum, Essen) a new voice, harsh and strident, unashamedly demotic, made itself heard across the mannered silence of contemporary abstract painting. Hence an ambiguity, due both to the abandonment of rhythmic contrasts giving a schematic unity to the picture (as in the early *Variations of Forms*, 1912-1914), and also to the juxtaposition of plastic elements differing in kind and indeed antagonistic: passages of flat color "enabling more rapid construction," and modeled forms "on which the eye can rest."[40] The resultant visual clash is rendered still more disconcerting by systematic contrasts of objects essentially incompatible with each other: living forms (faces, a torso, a human arm, a plant or fruit) and inanimate things (a plaster mask, a bottle, a screw, a hat,

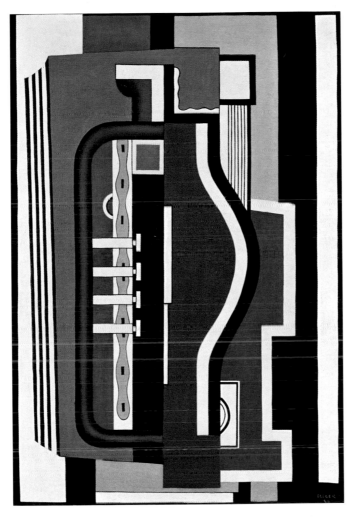

THE ACCORDION, 1926. STEDELIJK VAN ABBE MUSEUM, EINDHOVEN (HOLLAND).

MONNA LISA WITH KEYS, 1930. MUSÉE FERNAND LÉGER, BIOT.

a fruit-dish), all depicted with such exactitude as to make the generic antinomy between the two species of objects still more flagrant. Thus a second type of ambiguity joins forces with the first; each object, while retaining its natural function or utilitarian significance, seems oddly out of context and this "dialectic of contraries" gives rise to curious anomalies and transferences which might almost be described as "sub-realist."

This cult of the object-in-itself, while exalting its form, cramps the painter's imagination and, in preventing him from "creating what he sees," also forbids his immersing himself in the "penumbra of the dreaming psyche."[41] At the time when the visionary fervor of Surrealism was superseding dadaist nihilism, Léger's will to power and his incorrigible rationalism denied him access to the Marvelous. In stressing so ruthlessly the incompatibility of objects, his art now ran the risk of growing prosaic and, dedicated as he claimed to be to "sheer force," he could not, or would not, perceive the singular beauty that Lautréamont had discovered long before in "the chance encounter of a sewing machine and an umbrella on an operating table." However, from 1928 to 1930, he progressively discarded the compositional methods of Neo-Plasticism, freed the object from any precise context, and with deliberate bravado projected it into empty, undifferentiated space (*Monna Lisa with Keys*, 1930, Fernand Léger Museum, Biot, preceded by *Composition with Keys*, 1929, Private Collection, and followed by two variants, each named *Composition with Keys and an Umbrella*, 1932, Private Collections). These works mark a return to fully plastic forms and by the same token a discovery whose consequences Léger was to exploit systematically in the coming years.

THE FOREST, 1936. PRIVATE COLLECTION, PARIS.

A DYNAMIC IMAGINATION

The Root and the Tree

> The image of the root (provided it's *sincere*)
> reveals in our dreams all that binds us to mother
> earth. For all our forbears, without exception,
> were tillers of the soil.
>
> GASTON BACHELARD

For having the extreme audacity of painting, in *The Supper in the House of Levi*, a Moor's head alongside Christ's, Veronese was charged by the Inquisition with sacrilege. He based his defense on the exigencies of his art: the need for a dark patch (the Moor's head) beside a light one (the head of Christ). "We painters take the same liberties as poets and madmen," he said, and his judges had the good sense to acquit him.

It was a licence of the same order—a poetic licence—that led Léger to place the likeness of Monna Lisa, a captivating, cloud-borne form, like an image on a popular color print, alongside a bunch of massive keys, likewise suspended in mid-air. Sticklers for pictorial propriety would err if they read into this composition some scurrilous intent. Here the painter treats the world-famous picture simply as "an object like other objects." Whether he depicted a key, a woman or a machine, his visual approach remained the same, conditioned solely by a sense of plastic values. Long before a modern French writer declared that "there's nothing to choose between a screw-nut and a saint," [42] Léger was playing havoc with the hierarchy of subjective values; to his keen-sighted eyes an ordinary nail seemed quite as interesting as a face. The subject was by way of being supplanted by the object. "I've tried to free it (the object) completely and use it as a constructive value."[43] Today the poet Alain Bosquet voices the same idea no less emphatically:

Fellow objects, let's make clear our kinship,
Let each of us be replaceable by the next man
And let's pool, dear objects, our deepest ignorances.
Thanks to you I accept myself; within me
Your constant grumbling proves that you exist.
A world is born anew where the absurd is natural at last.

Léger had already conjured up a world where the absurd was natural when one day he found he needed "something totally different from the keys." It was then that he overstepped the bounds which Braque had set to the domain of painting —Braque who had once declared that "the painter does not try to re-create an anecdote, but to create a pictorial fact." The "dialectic of contraries" had breached the dikes; those contrasts of purely painterly data which had stood Veronese in good stead at his trial and had bulked so large in the *Variations of Forms* of the years 1912-1914, now gave place to contrasts of things, antinomies of categories. Thus plastic data largely superseded pictorial data and conferred on the object what Léger called its "dignity as an existing thing," with the result that the object now is treated as an abstract value, as little realistic as the hero of a Balzac novel, acquires more "character" than style, more forcefulness than grace, and takes on the exact hue of the painter's mood. Here, as Alain Bosquet also said, "we have prose that bites us to the quick."

It was not so much because from 1922 on Léger had resumed closer, more direct and constant contact with the countryside (he had inherited a farm in Normandy and was living at Fontenay-aux-Roses, in the Paris suburbs), as because at this time he began to find in the tree and the root a wonderfully rewarding

THE TREE IN THE LADDER, 1943-1944. MUSÉE FERNAND LÉGER, BIOT.

Lég. 36

ELEMENTS ON A BLUE GROUND, 1941. AIMÉ MAEGHT COLLECTION, PARIS.

theme—and he was often to revert to it. Examples are *Tree Trunks*, 1931, Louise Leiris Gallery, Paris; *The Forest*, 1936, and *Landscape*, 1936, in private collections, Paris; *The Tree in the Ladder*, 1943-1944, and *503*, 1943-1944, at Biot.

Naturally enough, the tree attracted him; it has always appealed to artists. He sensed "an animal force" in it. "Its branches have a dynamic violence. What a multitude of incredible forms, and what diversity! No two trees are alike. I remember seeing two plane-trees cut down, lying on the ground. It was a moonlight night and the spectacle was truly terrifying, devilish, nightmarish. They looked like slaughtered beasts and some of the branches were screaming with pain. Yet when at other times you look at trees, how superb is their placidity!... I never feel at peace when there are trees around me."[44]

That was literally true. Trees always had a disturbing influence on Léger, setting his psychic mechanism in motion, and galvanizing his imagination. In them he found a supreme embodiment of the clash of antagonistic forces. For the tree is a nucleus of contradictions. Whether standing or laid low,

> Dragging its slow weight along,
> Deformed from birth and gnarled, [45]

truncated, leafy or bare of foliage, bulky or slender, the tree is visualized by our waking dreamer as a plastic entity charged with inner contradictions and synthetic imagery. "The tree," as Gaston Bachelard has aptly said, "is an *integrating object*, usually a work of art *per se*."[46] For Léger it condensed the dream of power that always haunted his imagination. Moreover, it obviously answered to his desire to find a natural object embodying the stress of contraries, a unique and dramatic expression of the surging life force immanent in all things.

Yet even more potently than in the tree itself, it is in the root that the conflict of antinomies is mobilized. Arbiter and

WOMAN BATHING, 1931. LOUIS CARRÉ COLLECTION, PARIS.

source of life and death, a "rape of the earth," the root nurses in
darkness a secret aspiration to pierce the sky, and thrusts out
groping tentacles instinct with subtle power, delicately prehen-
sile, in all directions. Central or peripheric, serving as a pivot or
fanning out in radicles, the root figures again and again in
Léger's work, always by reason of his "taste for the object."[47]

From the purely plastic viewpoint, it acted as the starting point of a quest leading the artist, by way of the *Black Root* (1941, Maeght Collection, Paris), to pure signs (*Elements on a Blue Ground*, 1941, Maeght Collection, Paris, formerly Dotremont Collection, Brussels, model for the ceramic *Great Black and Red Branch*, 1951, Art Institute of Chicago). Here the sign is elastic, reduced to clean-cut masses of negative plena and positive voids—we are inevitably reminded of Arp's and Henry Moore's "essential" constructions, and indeed it is obvious that the pictorial architecture of *Polychrome Divers* (1942-1946, Biot) and *Acrobats in Grey* (1944, Biot) derives from them.

Embodying similar elements, that key work *Divers on a Yellow Background* (1941, Art Institute of Chicago) clearly indicates the transition now in progress: forms of human and forms of vegetable origin ring the changes on their pictorial functions, merging and dovetailing into each other as they fall into place, and integrate that "something abstract" which Virginia Woolf named "reality" into the world of the visible. In point of fact Léger had as early as 1931 produced a large composition which seems based less on a clash of two contending themes (life and death) than on a curious intermingling of genres and even genders. That sedately challenging *Woman Bathing* (Louis Carré Collection, Paris), in which the woman's body is rendered with such masterly freedom, derives its forcefulness, weight and vitality from the masculine element—the mutilated tree trunk— which itself, by a curious transference, is feminized. The body, with its sandy hue and the narrow, strongly marked bands of shadow on its contours, seems incorporated into the undulating soil. The broadly treated background planes reiterate, in successive waves, the ample rhythms of the massive body. And the whole landscape seems to be wilting under the blue intensity of a cloudless sky.

ANIMATED LANDSCAPE, 1921. PRIVATE COLLECTION, PARIS.

A REVERIE OF THE WILL

The Gazeless Man

> When the real is present in full force, in all its
> earthbound materiality, we may easily be led to
> think that the "function of the real" precludes
> the "function of the unreal." But this would
> mean forgetting all the unconscious urges,
> dream-begotten stimuli, forever active below
> the threshold of conscious life.
>
> GASTON BACHELARD

LÉGER had not always given such emphasis to the human figure
as in the phase we now shall deal with. Yet even when,
around 1920, he was fascinated by the possibilities of non-
figurative art, he still included the figure in two series of compositions (1920-1924) which unquestionably rank as landmarks in
his œuvre. This did not imply, as has often been said, a "return
to the human." The artist merely readjusted the focus of his
vision so as to gain a clearer view of man across the space and
rigid forms of the machine age.

It was now, about the time he was turning forty, that he
embarked on a series of "Animated Landscapes" in which he
believed he was "breaking away from civilization,"[48] and also
on a group of "Compositions with Large Figures" showing a
still surer sense of everyday reality. Both sequences express the
same *Weltanschauung*, reveal a similar will to synthesis, and
purport to convey the *vis inertiae* latent in static forms.

The "Animated Landscapes" (Private Collection, Paris;
Morton G. Neuman Collection, Chicago; C. Renault Collection,
Paris)—otherwise known as *Man with a Dog*, *The Fishermen*,
Repose, etc., all dated 1921—show a strict application of the

THREE WOMEN (LE GRAND DÉJEUNER), 1921. COLLECTION, THE MUSEUM
OF MODERN ART, NEW YORK. MRS SIMON GUGGENHEIM FUND.

compositional technique which culminated (1919-1920) in
The City. For celebrating the countryside of Normandy the
artist employs the same full-bodied signs. The layout is domi-
nated by verticals enclosing highly studied decorative contrasts.
Around the featureless man and the stylized animal undulate
the contours of a strip of land, a tree, a cactus-like plant, while
rectangular passages of flat color alternate with bright or dark

patches suggesting a farmhouse or a group of cottages. Thanks to an exceptionally sensitive handling of color, the artist brings off the feat of blending a real feeling for nature with the pictorial architecture of a highly personal variant of Constructivism.

That superb canvas *Mother and Child with a Dog* (1919-1920, Maeght Collection, Paris) acts, morphologically speaking, as a link between Léger's Norman landscapes and the impressive

WOMAN AND CHILD, 1922. KUNSTMUSEUM, BASEL.

series of "Doric" and horizontal compositions of which we seem to have intimations as early as 1919 in *Two Women with a Child* (Private Collection, France). In this work the artist brings into play the full powers of his maturity. Restored to its domestic milieu, the human figure—monumental, impassive, reduced to its most elementary power—comes into its own at the nadir of the mechanistic phase. And it falls aptly into place in an œuvre that might be described as one long dialogue between man and his technical environment. Drained of psychological content and any precise allusions to a personality—note that not only the features but the hands, too, are omitted—the figure exists *in vacuo*, in a limbo between the real and the unreal. Like Robert Musil's *Mann ohne Eigenschaften* it has no qualities, no soul, no name, no gaze. Standing for the nondescript "one" in such phrases as "One would think...," this is a being "relegated to the frozen void of impersonal existence, the man-in-the-street of our great cities, one of those interchangeable people who *are* nothing and look like nothing in particular. There are millions of them about, and they belong to the new species of man our age has brought into being."[19]

Among the pictures illustrating this approach mention may be made of *Three Women with Flowers*, 1920, Carré Collection, Paris; *Two Women holding a Bunch of Flowers*, 1921, Private Collection, France; *Le Déjeuner*, 1921, Private Collection, Paris; *The Readers*, 1924, Collection of Baronne Gourgaud, Paris; *Le Grand Déjeuner (Three Women)*, 1921, Museum of Modern Art, New York. Painted in the same year as Picasso's *Three Women at the Spring* (Museum of Modern Art, New York), this last work is not merely one which illustrates Léger's "grand style" in full fruition; it has a not unworthy place in the lineage of those masterpieces ranging from Fouquet's *Virgin* to Delacroix's *Women of Algiers* and *Odalisque with a Slave* which constellate the long history of French art. An unerring sense of order assures the

THREE WOMEN ON A RED GROUND, 1927.
FERNAND GRAINDORGE COLLECTION, LIÈGE.

balanced disposition of contrasted forms and passages of meticulously flat color. The inner edges of figures are fringed with zones of shadow, as though they were illuminated by the slanting rays of spotlights placed along the sides—and this is one of the devices characteristic of what we may call Léger's central style. The compromise between the plasticity of the two-dimensional figures and the handling of some objects (the tables for example) in inverted perspective gives the composition as a whole a spatial configuration of an exceptional type. Viewed in close-up, given the strictly frontal pose characteristic of archaic art, and built up of spheres and cylinders, with hair like bands of corrugated iron, these three women are starkly, almost brutally dehumanized.

In this context we must remember that Léger always regarded any attempt at psychological expression as "sentimental," and tried to treat the human figure as an object pure and simple, having exactly the same plastic qualities as those he so much appreciated in the machine.[50]

In another of his major works we find the same fine simplicity, and it is as flawlessly composed as a Poussin landscape or an Ingres interior. The *Woman and Child* (1922, Kunstmuseum, Basel) owes nothing to the normal way of seeing; rather, it is the product of an obscure reverie of the will. Here, again, circular formations rule out sentiment. The circle acts as a nucleus of force, and the tense rigidity of the line hints at restrained energy. The lack of any trace of living flesh deprives the bodies of individuality, even of any indication of age. Generalization has submerged particular cases and these figures join the ranks of the idola of the mechanistic world. There is no denying that these creatures made of billets of wood, their necks of steel rings and their hair of sheet metal remind us of robots; indeed they differ little from inanimate objects. Paradoxically enough, their setting of man-made forms seems more alive than they, and a uniform neutrality pervades the work, each line of which, each accent and each note of color falls into place with mathematical precision. The artist's consummate mastery of his medium makes the anatomy of a muscle, the feasibility of a gesture, the glint of an eye seem irrelevant, and compensates for the lack of any affective link between the woman and the child. Such a work as this needed an exceptional gift of co-ordination. Its magnificence tends to make us forget all the preliminary studies, the experiments and the hard thinking that must have gone to its making. For it implies a thorough understanding of that "reasoned unreason" which Paul Valéry held to be a *sine qua non* of artistic composition. Its layout is based on two lateral, asymmetrical coulisses providing vistas of an order more abstract than representational, more fictive than allusive, since departing from the "primitive" usage of such coulisses) they seem to project the background elements towards the center of the canvas. The body of the reclining woman in the foreground forms a sharply defined diagonal, which however does not impair the languorous immobility of her posture. On the left a thick-leaved plant links up the rhythms of the landscape with the straight lines of a chest of drawers, while the round mass of a vase serves the same purpose on the right. Everywhere horizontals neutralize the slanting lines conveying depth   so much so that all the picture elements fall into equilibrium along the vertical and seem to be straining forward, towards the space of the beholder.

BUTTERFLIES, 1937. GALERIE LOUIS CARRÉ, PARIS.

APOTHEOSIS OF THE SIGN

An Abbreviated World

It is this moment between town and country, this moment
Of grass and tiles, that signifies so well
That hinge of the century, that bridge
Between Corot and—what name will he have, our painter of total
It's this moment that is Léger.   [urbanization?

ARAGON

B ASIC to Léger's style is the sublime simplicity that he achieved quite early in his career. Simplicity is an inner wealth that calls for a long patience and absolute precision in the choice of the terms the painter uses for expressing the complexity of things. Thanks to this patience and precision, the form his message takes is all the clearer, more concise, more legible. That it may seem schematic, even uncouth, matters little, provided it is charged from the start with power, instinctual drive and keen intelligence. Charm was the least of the concerns of the painter of *Nudes in the Forest* and the *Grand Déjeuner (Three Women)*. For close on twenty years it was always himself that he depicted, and in accents so compelling that he had no need to announce his name. As he advanced from strength to strength, his eye acquired the lucidity of the clairvoyant. More and more he tightened his grasp, welding together the manifold phases and facets of his massive discourse.

It was in 1929, in *Two Figures with Flowers* (Private Collection, France), whose hieratic figures make us think of column-statues, that for the last time he kept to the spherical figurations that had characterized his "Doric" period (1920-1924). But this

COMPOSITION WITH THREE FIGURES, 1932.
MUSÉE NATIONAL D'ART MODERNE, PARIS.

key work synchronized with a series of works of quite another order, the "objects in space" (1928-1930). Note, too, that this picture was made subsequently to *Three Women on a Red Ground* (Fernand Graindorge Collection, Liège) in which already, in 1927, we find intimations of a wish to render force under

COMPOSITION WITH PARROTS, 1935-1939.
MUSÉE NATIONAL D'ART MODERNE, PARIS.

a new form. Here the ancient symbol of the circle seems to sag under the weight of heavy curves, though the style is no less grandiose, the insistence on plastic volume no less pronounced. This applies equally to another picture painted in 1927, *Nude on a Red Ground* (Madame Marie Cuttoli Collection, Paris). The primitive atmosphere of these works and their striking abbreviations remind us of the Selinus *Medea* and *The Blessed* in the tympanum of Sainte-Foy at Conques. Indeed we feel that across a gulf of time the genius of archaic and Romanesque art has returned, amazingly, to life, in all its rugged eloquence under the brush of this typically modern artist.

A remarkable feature of most of Léger's works in the 1920s is the scale of the pictorial construction and the size of details, no matter what their figural context and the dimensions of the work as a whole. All reveal the same obsession with the "close-up." It is obvious that the motion picture, which back in 1916 had made so strong an impression on him, played a major role in Léger's visual and aesthetic evolution. At the time when, under the influence of the object-sequences in Abel Gance's film *La Roue* (also perhaps of the theory of "cine-plastics" advanced by Elie Faure in 1920), he made the famous *Ballet Mécanique*, a film based wholly on a rhythmic flow of imagery, Léger all but abandoned painting. This was in or about 1925. The close-up had, as he admitted, "turned his head." "It's a diabolical invention! Did you know what a foot really *is* until you saw it come alive in a shoe under a table on the screen? It's as thrilling as a figure. A quite novel poetry, the poetry of the *transformed object*, is coming into the world and a new art will be built up on these new discoveries, this new truth." A dubious truth as things turned out, for thirty years later the cinema was to act on painting in a far more drastic manner, when Mark Rothko swept the canvas clear of the "picture" and used it as a support for free-flowing waves of light, a painting without objects—unless, indeed, the light evoked and manipulated by the artist may be described as an "object."

Surer than ever of painting "with his whole body," Léger decided around 1930 to make a complete synthesis of his discoveries, and feeling the need of elbow room, he once again

THE POLYCHROME DIVERS, 1942-1946. MUSÉE FERNAND LÉGER, BIOT.

BIG JULIE, 1945. COLLECTION, THE MUSEUM OF MODERN ART, NEW YORK.
ACQUIRED THROUGH THE LILLIE P. BLISS BEQUEST.

employed large canvases. *Composition with Three Figures* (Musée
d'Art Moderne, Paris; initial version, Madame Y. Zervos
Collection, Paris) inaugurated in 1932 that long imposing cycle
which was to culminate in 1945, with *Big Julie* (Museum of

Modern Art, New York). These works are monumental in the fullest sense; they have not only the essential grandeur that comes of architecturally ordered composition, but also a superb aloofness; they hold our gaze without stirring our emotions. In *Composition with Three Figures*, assembling women, pylons and cordage on a neutral plane without regard to scale, the artist exploited the procedure he had lit on when painting his *Monna Lisa with Keys*. Divided into two parts linked by a serpentine formation like a vegetable growth, the picture elements seem to float in an undifferentiated space. The women's arms are arched in graceful curves like those of dancers and the massive immobility of bodies in the earlier works gives place to rhythmic movement. A flowing, all-enveloping line (this too is new) defines and lightens forms, giving the human figure a suppleness hitherto absent in Léger's work. But the line is no more representational than it is in Matisse's compositions. It implements a spatial modulation marking transitions from angular design to dynamic arabesques and also enabling tonal gradations on their margins.

Two works are closely associated with this crucial period: *Marie the Acrobat* (1933, Louis Carré Collection, Paris, first state at Biot) and *Adam and Eve* (1934, first state at Biot). They, too, are based on a carefully worked-out contrast between two antithetic, well-defined themes. Later, we find a fusion taking place in the large *Composition with Parrots* (1935-1939, Musée d'Art Moderne, Paris; studies dated 1933 and 1937 at Biot), climax of this synthetic phase. A vertical arrangement of the masses and an alternation of filled and empty areas, of light and dark zones, is traversed by an undulating rhythm of counterbalanced curves setting the tempo of a ballet of supple, elastic signs poised in an imaginary space.

The figural associations of *Composition with Parrots* are dispensed with in *The Divers* (1941-1942, Museum of Modern

THE GREAT PARADE, 1954. COURTESY THE SOLOMON R. GUGGENHEIM MUSEUM, NEW YORK.

Art, New York), in which the dance of realistic forms gives place to a pageant of signs. Here the integration of elements of quite different origins is carried a stage farther; we are transported into a realm of pure imagination where two forms—the man and the root—are so inextricably interlocked that they seem to belong to the same genus, the same plastic world.

This work is not the harbinger of a new style; properly speaking, there is no "American period" in Léger's œuvre, nor did he change his viewpoint after moving to the United States (in 1940). The problem he set out to solve was that of combining the static energy of the plane, embodied in *The City* (1919-1920),

THE COUNTRY OUTING, 1954. AIMÉ MAEGHT COLLECTION, PARIS.

THE CONSTRUCTORS, 1950. MUSÉE FERNAND LÉGER, BIOT.

with the dynamism of the curve pervading the recent *Composition with Parrots*. With this in mind, he embarked on a series of variations on the theme of "men in space." For *Polychrome Divers* (1942-1946, Fernand Léger Museum, Biot) he conjured up memories of the youngsters he had seen plunging into the waters of Marseilles harbor when in October 1940 the ship in which he was going to New York was about to weigh anchor. Disarticulated, elongated, enlarged out of all proportion, fragments of the divers' bodies—a head, legs and arms—sink down along a vertical plane towards the depths, amid what look like footprints, in a saraband of positive and negative signs that flash out in all directions.

Here for the first time the new procedure which was to culminate in 1954 in two definitive works *The Great Parade* (Solomon R. Guggenheim Museum, New York) and *The Country Outing* (Aimé Maeght Collection, Paris), makes its appearance. Black, dense, emphatic line, winding its way *above* the colored zones, dominates the composition, while spacious passages of flat color traverse it *under* the design. Color no longer serves to clothe or fill out form, but is given complete independence vis-à-vis the line. This bold dichotomy leads to an abandonment of conventional modeling and points the way to startling abbreviations and an apotheosis of the sign. The procedure now adopted was fundamental to that dazzling homage to a personal friend, *Portrait of Paul Eluard* (1947, Private Collection, Paris). Tested out in 1942, in *The Dance* (Private Collection, France) and *Two Women with a Bird* (Louise Leiris Collection, Paris), it may have derived, if at a far remove, from a study of Gauguin's innovations. It is also quite possible that Léger got the idea of it from cubist *papiers collés*. But, allowing for these precedents, the ever-changing lights of Broadway were, on the painter's own showing, a more immediate source. "You are standing there talking to some one and suddenly he becomes blue. Then the color goes, another comes and he turns red or yellow. That color, the color of the flashing lights, is free, it's in space. I have tried to do the same thing in my canvases."[51]

However, on his return to France in December 1945, there comes, it seems, a decline in his imaginative power. Caught up in a life of action, his passion for "the real" neutralizes "the function of the unreal" and now he appears to content himself with assimilating, without trying to enlarge on, the discoveries of earlier years. Though he continues to turn out a steady flow of pictures, the execution is looser and the drawing heavier, as in *Leisure* (1948-1949, Musée d'Art Moderne, Paris). The subject now is tending to supersede the object. *The Constructors* (1950, Fernand Léger Museum, Biot) might seem to indicate a flagging of the artist's creative inspiration. Any such apprehension, however, is effectively dispelled by the amazing recovery of his full powers evidenced by that glorious synthesis of all his past achievements, *The Great Parade* (1954, final version in the Solomon R. Guggenheim Museum, New York), a definitive work in every sense, dating as it does to the last year of his life. "By ruthless application of the most absolute contrasts," the artist achieved that "maximum of power," without recourse to any spurious eloquence, which he had always aimed at. The human figure is a purely plastic element, and if it happens that a smile hovers on the lips of a clown, this "is not expression," the painter reminds us; "it's a trick of the trade *(métier)*." Once again a circle encloses the operative motif. "Nothing's as round as the circus," Léger pointed out. "It's a big basin in which circular forms are 'developed'... The ring dominates, swallows up everything... Visit the circus. You're escaping from your rectangles, your geometric windows, and entering the land of circles in action."[52]

Symbol of eternity, the circle is a promise of duration. Had Léger this in mind?

COLOR IN SPACE

A Walking Flower

It is in reality the diversity of things that
builds me up.

FRANCIS PONGE

WE have attempted to trace, amid the incessant flux of
parallel or superimposed themes, the steady development
of Léger's art, its sudden forward leaps and its premeditated
reversions to the past. At every stage it is apparent that the
painter's inspiration had its source in life, the more or less
mechanized life of countryfolk and cityfolk engaged in their
appointed tasks or enjoying well-earned leisure. Léger always
felt at ease with the working class and the professedly "extra-
social" art of the heyday of the French bourgeoisie had no
appeal for him.

Once he had found himself, the idea of taking a lead from
others never crossed his mind and, so far as his vision of the
world was concerned, he was in a sense the loneliest of the
artists of his generation. His creative zest never flagged, nor
did his bold defiance of the customary, would-be sacrosanct
ways of seeing. While claiming for himself the privilege of
sometimes making a mistake (apropos of *The Constructors*,
described as "an experiment," he said "I don't know if I've
brought it off, but it was a rumpus well worth provoking"), he
always made a point of rendering with scrupulous exactitude

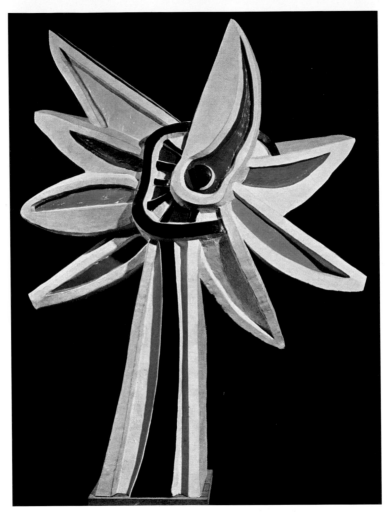

THE WALKING FLOWER, 1950. CERAMIC.
MUSÉE NATIONAL D'ART MODERNE, PARIS.

those relations between man and his natural or mechanized environment which were the constant theme of his creations.

The purely stylistic decline we seem to detect in his paintings of the years 1945-1954 was far from involving a repudiation of the basic principles of his art. During this period he explored what might be styled a side-line, in which he could exercise his natural gift for handicraft and which also helped him to recapture not only the pristine freshness of his early inspiration but also the precise forms and essential features of his canvases. In 1949, when Picasso had just begun producing ceramics at Vallauris, and Chagall at Vence, Léger tried his hand at this (for him) new form of art at Biot, a village in the Alpes-Maritimes, where one of his former pupils, Roland Brice, put his kilns at Léger's disposal. He had no desire to turn out utilitarian bric-à-brac or merely decorative objects. His program was more ambitious: that of associating the age-old techniques of the potter with the art of sculpture; of imposing on terracotta the dynamic line of *constructed* forms and launching into space, sometimes as an accompaniment to scenes of nature and sometimes as architectural adjuncts, plastic signs glazed in pure tones. Thus it was in polychrome sculpture in the round and bas-reliefs that he found a final outlet for the repertory of forms he had built up in his synthetic period and for his outstanding discoveries of the years 1930-1945.

Between 1932, when in *Composition with Three Figures* line was given free play, and 1939, the year in which the *Composition with Parrots* was completed, Léger had produced a series of pictures which, despite their themes and titles, can hardly be called still lifes, so profoundly modified are the relations between the natural objects they purport to render. In the sequence of "flowers and butterflies" we have a galaxy of signs, unmodeled forms elegantly poised in an often purely imaginary space, rendered in vivid, pure, full-bodied colors, bound with thin circumscribing lines and having black or white slab-like edges that recall Arp's pieces of wood cut into intriguing shapes (but without their sensual quality). In a butterfly's wing, a tiny petal, a canary's feather, enlarged out of all proportion, transposed or transfigured, all life is epitomized.

Here the close-up of the cinema is replaced by microscopic magnification; Léger is one of the few twentieth-century painters (along with Klee and Franz Marc) who realized and frankly admitted the debt contemporary vision owes to the microscope. Before applying these singular transformations to ceramic art he embodied them in a remarkable mural (planned in 1938) designed to "neutralize" an old-fashioned chimney-piece in the New York apartment of Nelson Rockefeller.

He had begun cautiously, "by taking his pictures as a starting point."[54] Or, perhaps, not so much his pictures as a group of forms having distinctive spatial functions *ab origine*, and he was at pains to keep their clarity and clean-cut line intact—for which reason he eschewed the risks of firing at a high temperature. Here once again we see the painter keeping to his "golden rule of contrasts." In the Musée d'Art Moderne in Paris, it governs the slow, finely balanced movement of *The Walking Flower*. It is a Léger that is passing before us—all limpid color and compelling power.

NOTES AND REFERENCES

[1] Quoted by Dora Vallier, *Cahiers d'Art*, Paris 1954, II, p. 134.

[2] Ibid., p. 135.

[3] Léger systematically destroyed his early canvases. A few scraps of information about them can be gleaned from Apollinaire. "I saw a few of Léger's early attempts in art. Bathing scenes at evening, a horizontal sea, with heads strewn here and there as in the difficult compositions that Matisse alone had ventured on." *(Les Peintres cubistes, Méditations esthétiques,* Paris 1913, reprinted by P. Cailler, Geneva 1950, p. 65).

[4] Quoted by Dora Vallier, *Cahiers d'Art*, Paris 1954, II, p. 140.

[5] Ibid., p. 149.

[6] F. T. Marinetti, *Le Futurisme*, E. Sansot, Paris 1911, pp. 180-186.

[7] Some remarks by Blaise Cendrars (who kept in close touch with Léger throughout his career) bear on the thorny question of influences and priorities. "While Picasso and Braque were being influenced, not to say perturbed, by the virtuosity of the theorists of the fourth dimension, Léger went on doggedly working, making so thorough a study of volumes and measures that he both gave rise to Russian Rayonnism as practised by Larionov and also had a direct influence on the best of the Italian futurist painters" *(Sélection,* Antwerp 1929, Cahier No. 5, p. 25).

[8] Delaunay made a discreet allusion to this influence. Cf. Robert Delaunay, *Du Cubisme à l'art abstrait, Documents inédits publiés par Pierre Francastel*, Paris 1957, pp. 74, 76 and 104. There exists in Paris (in a private collection) a sketch for *The Wedding* (measuring 32 ¼ by 26 ¾ inches); cf. the catalogue of the exhibition "Le Cubisme," Musée National d'Art Moderne, Paris 1953, No. 47.

[9] The first version of this picture, somewhat smaller (51 ½ by 39 inches), is in the Fernand Léger Museum, Biot. It throws a good deal of light on the painter's evolution.

[10] Cf. André Verdet, *Fernand Léger*, P. Cailler, Geneva 1955, pp. 14 and 72. Léger said much the same thing to Dora Vallier: "Delaunay and I flung ourselves into the battle of color. What we were attempting to do was the opposite of what they were doing in Montmartre. Delaunay wanted to paint in terms of the color relations employed by the Impressionists. I told him that they'd lead him up a blind alley, that he was doing no more than improve on Signac. But he kept hitting back at me: 'And what about you, with your local tones? You're going to take us back to museum art' " (op. cit., p. 149).

[11] Quoted by Dora Vallier, op. cit., p. 150.

[12] *Mercure de France*, October 16, 1912, pp. 894-895 (quoted in the catalogue of the exhibition "Le Cubisme," Musée national d'Art Moderne, Paris 1953, pp. 38-39).

[13] Cf. Pierre Francastel, *Peinture et Société*, Audin, Lyons 1952, p. 251.

[14] Guillaume Apollinaire, *Les Peintres cubistes*, pp. 68-69.

[15] R. Hoppe, *Cahiers d'Art*, Paris 1933, 3-4, p. 128.

[16] Quoted by Dora Vallier, op. cit., p. 140.

[17] It is worth while quoting the terms of this contract in full:

"Entre les soussignés Monsieur Fernand Léger, artiste-peintre, 13, rue de l'Ancienne Comédie, à Paris, et Monsieur Henry Kahnweiler, marchand de tableaux, 28, rue Vignon, à Paris, il a été convenu ce qui suit, pour une durée de trois ans, à partir du premier octobre 1913 (je dis dix-neuf cent treize):

"Monsieur Léger s'engage à vendre toute sa production à Monsieur Kahnweiler, et à ne rien vendre à qui que ce soit en dehors de lui. Il cède à Monsieur Kahnweiler les droits de reproduction de tout ce qu'il vendra.

"Monsieur Kahnweiler s'engage à acheter tout ce que Monsieur Léger produira de tableaux à l'huile ainsi qu'au moins 30 dessins rehaussés, 20 dessins au trait, aux prix ci-dessous:

toiles au-dessus de 120	500	fr.
" de 120	400	"
" de 100	300	"
" de 80 et de 60	250	"
" de 50	200	"
" de 40	150	"
" de 30	100	"
" de 25	75	"
toiles de 20, 15, 12, 10 et 8	50	"
dessins rehaussés	30	"
" au trait	15	"

"A Paris, le 20 octobre 1913."

[18] From a typescript, p. 12 (quoted in the catalogue of the exhibition "Le Cubisme," Musée National d'Art Moderne, Paris, pp. 45-46).

[19] Cf. *Cahiers d'Art*, Paris 1933, 3-4, p. 115.

[20] Quoted by Pierre Descargues, *Fernand Léger*, Editions du Cercle d'Art, Paris 1955, p. 37.

[21] Quoted by Douglas Cooper, *Fernand Léger*, Editions des Trois Collines, Geneva 1949, p. 74.

[22] Some sketches made at the front (1915-1916) are preserved at Biot.

[23] Observations of this kind (and many others) could be added to a dossier preliminary to a "History of Modern Sensibility"—which remains to be written.

[24] Fernand Léger, *L'Esthétique de la machine*, Sélection, Antwerp 1923, p. 374.

[25] Gilbert Simondon, *Du mode d'existence des objets techniques*, Aubier, Paris 1959, p. 12; G. Friedmann, *Réévaluation des sociétés modernes*, Diogène, 31, Paris 1960, p. 63.

[26] Gilbert Simondon, op. cit., p. 197.

[27] André Chastel, *Le Jeu et le Sacré dans l'art moderne*, Critique, 97, Paris, pp. 520-521.

[28] Jacques Vaché, quoted by André Chastel, op. cit., p. 529.

[29] Gilbert Simondon, op. cit., p. 11.

[30] Maurice Blanchot, *L'Espace littéraire*, Gallimard, Paris 1955, p. 40.

[31] Ibid.

[32] Nikolaus Pevsner, *Les Sources du XXᵉ siècle*, Editions de la Connaissance, Brussels 1961, p. 260.

[33] Quoted by Dora Vallier, op. cit., p. 161.

[34] *Le paysage dans l'œuvre de Léger*, Editions Louis Carré, Paris 1956, p. 26.

[35] Le Corbusier, *L'Architecture et Fernand Léger*, Sélection, Antwerp 1929, Cahier No. 5, p. 23.

[36] Ibid., p. 24.

[37] Quoted by Douglas Cooper, op. cit., p. 91.

[38] Ibid., p. 92.

[39] Le Corbusier, op. cit., p. 24.

[40] Fernand Léger, in *Cahiers d'Art*, II, Paris 1954, p. 152.

[41] Gaston Bachelard, *Poétique de la rêverie*, Presses Universitaires de France, Paris 1960, p. 15.

[42] Alain Bosquet, *A l'impératif*, Cahiers des Saisons, No. 29, 1962, p. 486.

[43] Preface to the catalogue of the Léger exhibition, Palais des Beaux-Arts, Brussels 1938.

[44] Quoted by Dora Vallier, op. cit., p. 140.

[45] A. Lubin, *Mon arbre chante*, Cahiers des Saisons, No. 29, 1962, p. 463.

[46] Gaston Bachelard, *La terre et les rêveries du repos*, Corti, Paris 1948, p. 299.

[47] *Le paysage dans l'œuvre de Léger*, op. cit., p. 35.

[48] Ibid., p. 34.

[49] Maurice Blanchot, *Le livre à venir*, N.R.F., Paris 1959, p. 172.

[50] Quoted by Dora Vallier, op. cit., p. 153.

[51] Ibid., p. 154.

[52] Fernand Léger, *Le Cirque*, Tériade, Paris 1949.

[53] Quoted by Maria Luz, *XXᵉ Siècle*, January 1952, p. 68.

[54] Quoted by André Verdet, *Fernand Léger*, Cailler, Geneva 1955, p. 88.

BIBLIOGRAPHY

A comprehensive bibliography was first compiled in 1949 by Hannah B. Muller, Librarian of the Museum of Modern Art, New York, for the book by Douglas Cooper, *Fernand Léger et le nouvel espace* (Editions des Trois Collines, Geneva 1949). This was brought up to date in Katherine Kuh's monograph, *Léger* (Art Institute of Chicago, 1953) and again in François Mathey's *Catalogue Fernand Léger, 1881-1955* (Musée des Arts Décoratifs, Paris 1956). For all publications issued prior to 1956 the reader is referred to these standard works. Below, under the headings "General Works" and "Magazine and Newspaper Articles," we confine ourselves to listing the principal items published since 1956, together with a few titles overlooked in the above-mentioned bibliographies. Any remaining gaps in our documentation will soon be filled by the archives now being set up at the Fernand Léger Museum, Biot. The Museum staff is also at work on a catalogue raisonné of Léger's entire œuvre.

Sources: Writings and Statements by the Artist

Les origines de la peinture contemporaine et sa valeur expressive, Montjoie, No. 8, Paris, May 29, 1913, p. 7; No. 9-10, June 14-29, 1913, pp. 9-10. — *Les réalisations picturales actuelles,* Soirées de Paris, June 15, 1914, No. 25, pp. 349-356. — *Pensées,* Valori Plastici, Rome, February-March 1919, No. 2-3, p. 2; Sélection, Antwerp, September 15, 1920, No. 2, p. 4. — *La couleur dans la vie,* Promenoir, Lyons 1921, No. 5, pp. 66-67. — *L'esthétique de la machine; l'objet fabriqué, l'artisan et l'artiste,* Der Querschnitt, Berlin 1923, vol. 3, pp. 122-129; Bulletin de l'Effort Moderne, Paris, January 1924, pp. 5-7; Sélection, Antwerp, February 1924, pp. 374-382. — *Kurzgefaßte Auseinandersetzung über das aktuelle künstlerische Sein,* Das Kunstblatt, Berlin 1923, vol. 7, pp. 1-4. — *Correspondance* (with Léonce Rosenberg), Bulletin de l'Effort Moderne, Paris, April 1924, No. 4, pp. 10-12. — *Réponse à une enquête: où va la peinture moderne?,* Bulletin de l'Effort Moderne, Paris, February 1924, p. 5. — *Réponse à une enquête sur le cubisme,* Bulletin de la Vie artistique, Paris, Novembre 1924, p. 486. — *Le Spectacle,* Bulletin de l'Effort Moderne, Paris, July 1924, pp. 4-7; October 1924, pp. 5-9; November 1924, pp. 7-9. — *Le Ballet-Spectacle: l'objet-spectacle,* Bulletin de l'Effort Moderne, Paris, February 1925, pp. 7-9. — *Sur le cinéma,* Les Cahiers du Mois, Paris 1925. — *Vive Relâche,* Bulletin de l'Effort Moderne, Paris, March 1925, pp. 5-7. — *Les Bals populaires,* Bulletin de l'Effort Moderne, Paris, February 1925, pp. 9-10; March 1925, pp. 4-5. — *Conférence sur l'Esthétique de la machine,* in Florent Fels, *Propos d'Artistes,* Paris 1925, pp. 98-106. — *Peinture et cinéma,* Paris 1925, pp. 107-108. — *Notations on Plastic Values,* catalogue of the Léger Exhibition, Anderson Galleries, New York 1925. — *A New Realism - the Object, its Plastic and Cinematographic Value,* Little Review, New York 1926,

No. 2, pp. 7-8. — *La peinture murale, la technique*, in Maurice Raynal, *Anthologie de la Peinture en France de 1906 à nos jours*, Paris 1927, pp. 205-206. — *La vue : objets, spectacles*, Cahiers de la République des Lettres, des Sciences et des Arts, Paris 1928, vol. XII, pp. 102-104. — *Meine Berliner Ausstellung*, Der Querschnitt, Berlin 1928, vol. 8, No. 1, pp. 35-37.—*Actualités*, Variétés, Brussels, January 15, 1929, pp. 522-525. — *Pensées sur l'art*, in W. George, *Fernand Léger*, Paris 1929, p. 14. — *De l'art abstrait*, Cahiers d'Art, Paris 1931, No. 3, pp. 151-152. — *New York vu par Fernand Léger*, Cahiers d'Art, Paris 1931, No. 9-10, pp. 437-439. — *A propos du cinéma*, Plans, Paris, January 1931, pp. 80-84. — Introduction to the catalogue of the Calder Exhibition, Galerie Percier, Paris 1931. — *Chicago*, Plans, Paris 1932, No. 11, pp. 63-68. — *Discours aux architectes*, Quadrante, Milan, September 1933, pp. 44-47. — *Chez Fernand Léger*, Beaux-Arts, Paris, April 21, 1933, pp. 1-2. — *L'art est entré en cambrioleur*, Mouvement, Paris 1933, No. 1, pp. 17-18. — *A propos du cinéma*, Cahiers d'Art, Paris 1933, 3-4, p. 133. —*Le Beau et le Vrai*, Beaux-Arts, Paris, February 9, 1934, p. 2. — *The New Realism*, Art Front, New York, December 1935, No. 8, pp. 10-11. — *Réponse à une enquête sur l'art d'aujourd'hui*, Cahiers d'Art, Paris 1935, No. 1-4, pp. 64-66. — *Pity Us!*, Art Digest, New York, October 15, 1935, p. 26. — *La couleur et le sentiment*, Pour Vous, Paris, September 1935, No. 358. — *Réponse à une enquête : Que feriez-vous si vous aviez à organiser l'Exposition de 1937?*, Vu, Paris 1935, No. 387, p. 1102. — *Où va la peinture?*, Commune, Paris, May 1935, pp. 944-946. — *Le nouveau réalisme*, in *La querelle du réalisme*, Paris 1936, pp. 73-79, 165-167. — *Painting and Reality*, Transition, New York 1936, No. 25, pp. 104-108. — *A Propos of Colour*, Transition, New York 1937, No. 26, p. 8. — *Sur la peinture*, in *L'Exposition 1937 et les Artistes à Paris*, Paris 1937, pp. 20-29. — *L'Art mural de Victor Servranckx*, Clarté, Brussels 1937, No. 7, pp. 20-21. — *Beauty in Machine Art*, Design, Columbus, Ohio, March 1938, pp. 6-7. — *Revival of Mural Art*, The Listener, London 1938, No. 450, pp. 403-409. — Preface to the catalogue of the Léger Exhibition, Brussels, Palais des Beaux-Arts, 1938. *Couleur dans le monde*, Europe, special issue devoted to *L'homme, la technique et la nature*, 1938, No. 185, pp. 99-113. — *Réponse à une enquête : l'acte créateur se ressent-il de l'influence des événements environnants?*, Cahiers d'Art, 1939, No. 1-4, pp. 70-72. — *The Question of Truth*, Architectural Forum, New York, February 1939, pp. 138-141. — *New York-Paris, Paris-New York*, La Voix de France, September 15, 1941, p. 10. — *Un art nouveau sous le ciel californien*, La Voix de France, November 1, 1941, p. 8. — *Découvrir l'Amérique*, La Voix de France, May 15, 1942, p. 9. — *Byzantine Mosaics and Modern Art*, Magazine of Art, Washington, April 1944, pp. 144-145. — *Relationship between Modern Art and Contemporary Industry*, in *Modern Art in Advertising : an Exhibition of Designs for Container Corporation of America*, Chicago, Art Institute, 1945, pp. 4-5. — *A propos du corps humain considéré comme un objet*, in *Fernand Léger*, Montreal 1945, pp. 63-75. — *L'œil du peintre*, Variétés, Paris 1945, No. 3. — *Modern Architecture and Color*, in *American*

Abstract Artists, New York 1946, pp. 34-35, 37-38. — *Causerie sur l'Art*, Arts de France, Paris 1946, No. 6, pp. 36-42. — *L'avenir est à la couleur*, Ecran français, Paris, April 3, 1946, p. 11. — *L'Amérique, c'est un monde*, Arts, Paris, January 4, 1946, pp. 1-2; Architectural Forum, New York, April 1946, pp. 50, 54, 58, 62. — *Le Peuple et les Arts*, Bulletin de "Travail et Culture", Paris, June-July 1946, pp. 35-36. — *L'art abstrait*, Cahiers des Amis de l'Art, Paris 1947, No. 11, p. 48. — *F. Léger, Interview par P. Descargues*, Arts, Paris, January 2, 1948, pp. 1-5. — *F. Léger et ses élèves vont décorer l'Exposition Internationale des Femmes*, Arts, Paris, May 28, 1948. — *Doit-on réformer l'enseignement des Beaux-Arts?*, Traits, Paris 1948, 4, pp. 1-8. — *Color in Architecture*, in S. Papadaki, *Le Corbusier*, New York 1948, pp. 78-80. — *Que Signifie: Etre témoin de son temps?*, Arts, Paris, March 11, 1949. — *Un nouvel espace en architecture*, Art d'Aujourd'hui, Boulogne 1949, No. 3, p. 19; autograph text reproduced in facsimile in F. H. Man, *Eight European Artists*, London 1954, Ch. 3. — *L'Art abstrait*, Derrière le Miroir, Paris 1949, No. 20-21, p. 9. — *Le Cirque*, Tériade, Paris 1949. — *Calder*, Derrière le Miroir, Paris 1950, No. 31, p. 7. — *Situation de la Peinture dans le temps actuel*, Biennale, Venice 1951, No. 5, p. 19. — *L'architecture moderne et la couleur*, Formes et Vie, Paris 1951, No. 1, pp. 24-26. — *Jamais de la vie je n'irai dans le Midi*, Arts, Paris, July 10, 1952, p. 10. — *Réponse à une enquête: l'art et le climat visuel contemporain*, catalogue of the Salon de Mai, Paris 1952, p. 1. — *Le problème de l'espace mural*, XXᵉ Siècle, January 1952, pp. 67-68. — *La Peinture moderne devant le monde actuel*, Les Lettres françaises, Paris, March 1952, No. 13, pp. 1, 9. — *Comment je conçois la figure*, in *La figure dans l'œuvre de Léger*, Galerie Carré, Paris 1952, pp. 29-33. — *Sens de l'art moderne*, Zodiaque, Saint-Léger-Vauton, No. 18-19, pp. 37-40. — *Réflexions sur l'intégration de la peinture et de la sculpture dans l'architecture*, I Quattro Soli, Turin 1954, No. 1, p. 8. — *Vers l'architecture*, exhibition catalogue, Galerie Carré, Paris 1953. — *Interview de M. Marceau*, Magnum, Frankfort 1954, No. 3. — *La vie fait l'œuvre de Fernand Léger*, statements quoted by Dora Vallier, Cahiers d'Art, II, 1954, pp. 133-172. — *Comment cela commence*, Les Lettres françaises, August 25, 1955. — *Les mains des constructeurs*, poem, Heures Claires, Paris 1955, No. 123, pp. 18-19. — *Polychromie architecturale*, Aujourd'hui, Paris 1955, No. 2. — Preface to *Fernand Léger*, monograph by Pierre Descargues, Paris 1955. — *Entretien de Fernand Léger avec Blaise Cendrars et Louis Carré sur le paysage dans l'œuvre de Léger*, L. Carré, Paris, 1956. — *Lettre à un ami*, Quadrum, Brussels, 1956 No. 2, pp. 77-79. — *La couleur dans l'architecture*, in *Problèmes de la Couleur*, Paris 1957, pp. 135-154. — J. CHARPIER and P. SEGHERS, *L'Art de la Peinture*, Paris 1957, pp. 623-627 (résumé of statements quoted by Dora Vallier). — *Le spectacle, lumière, couleur, image mobile, objet-spectacle*, Aujourd'hui, Paris 1948, No. 1-7, pp. 44-45 (reprinted from Bulletin de l'Effort moderne, October 1924, No. 8). — *Mes Voyages*, Paris 1960.

Historical Background

F. T. Marinetti, *Le Futurisme*, Paris 1911. — G. Apollinaire, *Les Peintres cubistes*, Paris 1913 (reprinted Geneva 1950, pp. 65-69). — A. J. Eddy, *Cubists and Post-Impressionism*, Chicago 1914. — P. Mondrian, *Le Néo-plasticisme*, Paris 1920. — Daniel Henry (Kahnweiler), *Der Weg zum Kubismus*, Munich 1920. — P. E. Küppers, *Der Kubismus*, Leipzig 1920. — E. Faure, *L'Arbre d'Eden*, Paris 1922, pp. 249-276. — Le Corbusier, *L'art décoratif d'aujourd'hui*, Paris 1925 (reprinted 1959), pp. 105-115. — A. Ozenfant and E. Jeanneret (Le Corbusier), *La Peinture moderne*, Paris 1927. — L. Moholy-Nagy, *The New Vision*, New York 1928 (3rd edition 1946, p. 34). — C. Pavolini, *Cubismo, futurismo, espressionismo*, Bologna 1929. — C. Zervos, *Histoire de l'art contemporain*, Paris 1930. — A. Ozenfant and J. Hodler, *Foundations of Modern Art*, London 1931. — P. Valéry, *Regards sur le monde actuel*, Paris 1931. — R. Huyghe, *Histoire de l'art contemporain*, Paris 1936, pp. 213-214. — A. H. Barr, *Cubism and Abstract Art*, New York 1936. — Le Corbusier, *Le lyrisme des temps nouveaux et l'architecture*, Colmar 1939. — B. Champigneulle, *L'inquiétude dans l'art d'aujourd'hui*, Paris 1939, pp. 129-130. — G. Keepes, *Language of Vision*, Chicago 1944 (2nd edition 1951). — E. Bonfante and J. Ravenna, *Arte cubista*, Venice 1945. — G. Friedmann, *Problèmes humains du machinisme industriel*, Paris 1946. — G. Bazin, *Le crépuscule des images*, Paris 1946, pp. 66-71. — P. M. Schuhl, *Machinisme et philosophie*, Paris 1947. — J. S. Schapiro, *Modern and Contemporary European History*, Boston 1946. — L. Moholy-Nagy, *Vision in Motion*, Chicago 1947, p. 132-133. — P. Eluard, *Voir*, Geneva 1948. — S. Giedion, *Mechanization Takes Command*, New York 1948. — G. Bachelard, *La terre et les rêveries de la volonté*, Paris 1948. — G. Bachelard, *La terre et les rêveries du repos*, Paris 1948. — G. Plekhanov, *L'art et la vie sociale*, Paris 1949. — G. Habasque, *Cubisme et phénoménologie*, Revue d'Esthétique, Paris, April-June 1949. — J. Cassou, *Situation de l'art moderne*, Paris 1950. — D. H. Kahnweiler, *Les années héroïques du cubisme*, Paris 1950. — L. Venturi, *Pour comprendre la peinture : de Giotto à Chagall*, Paris 1950. — G. Friedmann, *Où va le travail humain?*, Paris 1950. — K. Kuh, *Art Has Many Faces*, New York 1951, p. 146. — A. Einstein and L. Infeld, *L'évolution des idées en physique*, Paris 1951. — R. Jeanne and C. Ford, *Histoire encyclopédique du cinéma*, Paris 1947-1952. — W. Hofmann, *Le maniérisme du XVIe siècle et l'art moderne*, Actes du XVIIe Congrès International d'Histoire de l'Art, Amsterdam 1952, pp. 545-550. — P. Francastel, *Peinture et Société*, Lyons 1952, p. 244. — H. Lefebvre, *Contribution à l'esthétique*, Paris 1953. — J. Gebser, *Ursprung und Gegenwart*, Stuttgart 1953, p. 316. — R. Cogniat, *Questo è il cubismo*, Arti, 1954, No. 1-2, pp. 20-22. — P. Ginestier, *Le Poète et la machine*, Paris 1954. — C. P. Bru, *Esthétique de l'abstraction*, Paris 1955. — B. Zevi, *Storia dell'architettura moderna*, Milan 1955, p. 41. — M. Blanchot, *L'espace littéraire*, Paris 1955. — A. Chastel, *Le Jeu et le Sacré dans l'art moderne*,

Critique, 1955, XI, pp. 428-446, 515-533. — P. M. LAPORTE, *Cubismo e scienza*, Sele Arte, March-April 1955, No. 17, pp. 20-33. — E. PANOFSKY, *Meaning in the Visual Arts*, New York 1955. — P. FRANCASTEL, *Art et Technique*, Paris 1956, p. 161. — G. KEEPES, *The New Landscape in Art and Science*, Chicago 1956. — P. FRANCASTEL, *Estève*, Paris 1956, pp. 26-27. — R. DELAUNAY, *Du Cubisme à l'art abstrait, Documents inédits réunis par P. Francastel*, Paris 1957, pp. 38, 73, 76, 93, 102, 140, 153, 223, 241. — G. PICON, *Panorama des idées contemporaines*, Paris 1957. — G. DUBY and R. MANDROU, *Histoire de la civilisation française*, Paris 1958, II, p. 285. — G. SIMONDON, *Du mode d'existence des objets techniques*, Paris 1958. — F. GILSON, *Peinture et réalité*, Paris 1958. — J. ULLMO, *La pensée scientifique moderne*, Paris 1958. — W. BENJAMIN, *Oeuvres choisies*, Paris 1959. — F. LOMBARDI, *Naissance du monde moderne*, Paris 1958. — J. SIMIAND, *Méthode historique et science sociale*, Annales, January-February 1960, pp. 83-119. — J. LAUDE, *Du cubisme à l'art abstrait*, Critique, May 1960, pp. 426-451. — G. FRIEDMANN, *Réévaluation des sociétés modernes*, Diogène, 1960, No. 31, pp. 62-74. — G. APOLLINAIRE, *Chroniques d'art (1902-1918)*, Paris 1960, pp. 373-374. — R. BANHAM, *Theory and Design in the First Machine Age*, London 1960, pp. 203-210. — U. ECO, *L'œuvre ouverte et la poétique de l'Indétermination*, N.R.F., Paris 1961, No. 91, pp. 117-124; No. 92, pp. 313-320. — M. PIETSCH, *Die industrielle Revolution*, Freiburg 1961. — D. H. KAHNWEILER, *Mes galeries et mes peintres. Entretiens avec Francis Crémieux*, Paris 1961. — G. POULET, *Les métamorphoses du cercle*, Paris 1961. — G. PICON, *D'une esthétique contemporaine*, Cahiers du Sud, 1961, No. 361, pp. 339-356. — M. MERLEAU-PONTY, *L'œil et l'esprit*, Les Temps Modernes, 1961, No. 184-185, pp. 193-227.

Monographs

M. RAYNAL, *Fernand Léger, vingt tableaux*, Ed. de l'Effort moderne, Paris 1920. — E. TÉRIADE, *Fernand Léger*, Ed. des Cahiers d'Art, Paris 1928. — W. GEORGE, *Fernand Léger*, Gallimard, Paris 1929. — J. BAZAINE, *Fernand Léger, peintures antérieures à 1940*, L. Carré, Paris 1945. — M. A. COUTURIER, M. GAGNON, S. GIEDION, F. HERTEL, S. KOOTZ, J. J. SWEENEY, *Fernand Léger, La forme humaine dans l'espace*, Editions de l'Arbre, Montreal 1945. — F. ELGAR, *Léger, Peintures, 1911-1948*, Editions du Chêne, Paris 1948. — D. COOPER, *Fernand Léger et le nouvel espace*, Editions des Trois Collines, Geneva 1949. — C. ROY, *Les Constructeurs*, Falaize, Paris 1951. — C. ZERVOS, *Fernand Léger, œuvres de 1905 à 1952*, Ed. des Cahiers d'Art, Paris 1952. — André MAUROIS, *Mon ami Léger*, L. Carré, Paris 1952. — M. JARDOT, *Dessins*, Editions des Deux Mondes, Paris 1953. — K. KUH, *Léger*, The Art Institute of Chicago 1953. — F. ELGAR, *Picasso et Léger, Deux hommes, deux mondes*, Les Amis de l'Art, Paris 1954. — P. DESCARGUES, *Fernand Léger*, Cercle d'Art, Paris 1955. — A. VERDET, *Fernand Léger, Le dynamisme pictural*, P. Cailler, Geneva 1955. — A. VERDET, *Fernand*

Léger. Images de R. Doisneau et G. Ehrman, R. Kister, Geneva 1956. —
M. JARDOT, *Fernand Léger*, Hazan, Paris 1956. — A. VERDET, *Fernand Léger, Bekenntnisse, Gespräche*, Die Arche, Zurich 1957. — *Fernand Léger*, in the series "Propos et Présence," Gonthier-Seghers, Paris 1959.

General Works

M. RAYNAL, *Anthologie de la peinture en France de 1906 à nos jours*, Paris 1927, pp. 205-212; in English, *Modern French Painters*, New York 1928. —
C. EINSTEIN, *Die Kunst des 20. Jahrhunderts*, Berlin 1926 (2nd edition, 1928, pp. 94-100). — R. ESCHOLIER, *La peinture française, XXe siècle*, Paris 1937, pp. 94-95. — B. DORIVAL, *Les étapes de la peinture française contemporaine*, Paris 1944, II, pp. 264-275. — A. LHOTE, *Traité du paysage*, Paris 1946, p. 95. — B. DORIVAL (editor), *Les peintres célèbres*, Geneva 1948, pp. 334-335. — R. HUYGHE, *Les contemporains*, Paris 1949, p. 63. — N. PEVSNER, *Pioneers of Modern Design from William Morris to Gropius*, New York 1949.
— M. RAYNAL and others, *History of Modern Painting*, Vol. III: *From Picasso to Surrealism*, Geneva 1950, pp. 72-75. — J. ROMERO BREST, *La pintura europea contemporánea, 1900-1950*, Buenos Aires 1952, pp. 127-138.
— M. RAYNAL, *Modern Painting*, Geneva 1953, pp. 156-157. — S. GIEDION, *Space, Time and Architecture*, Cambridge (Mass.) 1954, pp. 473, 548, 567. —
C. ROGER-MARX, *Maîtres du XIXe siècle et du XXe*, Paris 1954, pp. 240-241. — *Dictionnaire de la Peinture moderne*, Paris 1954 (article by F. Elgar, pp. 153-156). — Felix H. MAN, *Eight European Artists*, London 1954, Ch. 3. — A. H. BARR, *Masters of Modern Art*, New York 1954, pp. 84-85, 96-97. — *Les Clés de l'art moderne*, Paris 1955, pp. 166-168. — H. SEDLMAYR, *Die Revolution der modernen Kunst*, Hamburg 1955, p. 128. —
W. HAFTMANN, *Malerei im 20. Jahrhundert*, Munich 1955, II, p. 136. —
B. DORIVAL, *Images de la peinture française*, Paris, n.d., pp. 99-100.
— P. DESCARGUES, *Le cubisme*, Paris 1956, p. 62. — P. FRANCASTEL, *Histoire de la peinture française*, Paris Brussels 1956, II, pp. 137 138, 150 151.
— F. FOSCA, *Bilan du cubisme*, Paris 1956, p. 52. — W. HOFMANN, *Zeichen und Gestalt. Die Malerei des 20. Jahrhunderts*, Frankfort 1957, pp. 91-93. —
B. DORIVAL, *La peinture du XXe siècle*, Paris 1957; in English, *Twentieth Century Painting*, New York 1958. — A. DE RIDDER, *De levende Kunst gezien te Venetie; XXIV Biennale 1948, XXV Biennale 1950, XXVI Biennale 1952, XXVII Biennale 1954, XXVIII Biennale 1956*, Brussels 1958, pp. 259-262. — M. GIEURE, *La peinture moderne*, Paris 1958, p. 73.
M. SEUPHOR, *Dictionnaire de la peinture abstraite*, Hazan, Paris 1957, pp. 46-48. — J. E. CIRLOT, *Arte contemporáneo*, Barcelona 1958. — S. CHENEY, *The Story of Modern Art*, London 1958. — C. McCURDY, *Modern Art, A Pictorial Anthology*, New York 1958. — P. COURTHION, *L'art indépendant. Panorama international de 1900 à nos jours*, Paris 1958, pp. 90-92.
— M. GIEURE, *La peinture moderne*, Paris 1958, pp. 73-74. — M. RAGON, *Le livre de l'architecture moderne*, Paris 1958, pp. 57-59. — G. BUFFET-PICABIA,

Aires abstraites, Geneva 1958. — M. Jean, *Histoire de la peinture surréaliste,* Paris 1959, p. 26. — W. Hofmann, *De Schilderkunst van de twintigste eeuw,* Utrecht 1959, pp. 97-99. — G. Habasque, *Cubism,* Geneva 1959, pp. 100-105. — H. Casteur and A. Smeets, *Inleiding tot de hedendaagse schilderkunst,* Bruges 1959, pp. 158-160. — L. Hautecœur, *Histoire de l'art,* Paris 1959, III, p. 310. — F. Mourlot, *Les Affiches originales des maîtres de l'école de Paris,* Paris 1959. — B. Majorick, *Ontwerpen en Verwerpen,* Amsterdam 1959, pp. 133-140. — H. Read, *A Concise History of Modern Painting,* London 1959, pp. 86-90. — J. Cassou, *Panorama des arts plastiques contemporains,* Paris 1960, pp. 228-236, pp. 271-275, etc. — J. Chapiro, *La ruche,* Paris 1960, pp. 55-59. — P. Lherminier, *L'art du cinéma,* Paris 1960, pp. 51, 430. — R. Rosenblum, *Der Kubismus und die Kunst des 20. Jahrhunderts,* Teufen 1960, pp. 126-148. — L. Zahn, *Kleine Geschichte der modernen Kunst,* Berlin 1961, p. 154. — J. Cassou, E. Langui, N. Pevsner, *Les sources du XXe siècle,* Brussels 1961, p. 52, etc.

Newspaper and Magazine Articles

E. L. T. Mesens, *"La création du monde" de Darius Milhaud,* Sélection, I, 1923, pp. 228-230. — C. Bernard, *F. Léger,* L'indépendance belge, May 18, 1938. — J. Lassaigne, *Le retour de Léger,* Panorama des Arts, 1946, Paris 1947, pp. 78-79. — M. A. Couturier, *L'église d'Assy,* L'Art sacré, 1-2, pp. 3-7. — A. S., *L'église d'Audincourt,* L'Art sacré, 1951, 3-4, pp. 20-23. — M. A. Couturier, *Aunque es de noche,* L'Art sacré, 1951, 3-4, pp. 10-18. — J. Bazaine, *Notes,* L'Art sacré, 1951, 3-4, pp. 24-26. — R. de Solier, *Kyrklig Konst i Frankrike,* Konstrevy, 1951, pp. 240-249. — F. Towarnicki, *En Provence retour aux arts du feu,* Plaisir de France, 1952, No. 171, pp. 36-40. — M. Raynal, *Montmartre au temps du "Bateau-Lavoir",* Médecine de France, 1952, No. 35, pp. 17-30. — R. Cogniat, *Tendances du décor de théâtre,* Art et Décoration, 1952, No. 30, pp. 1-6. — Dom A. Surchamp, *Un art sacré pour notre temps,* Zodiaque, 1952, No. 11, pp. 3-35. — F. Marshall, *The Artists and the Ballet,* Studio, 1952, 144, pp. 161-167. — W. George, *Les sculptures polychromes de F. Léger,* Art et Industrie, 1952, No. 24, pp. 44-45. — P. Haesaert, *A la recherche de l'espace,* XXe Siècle, 1952, No. 2, pp. 13-26. — C. Zervos, *Coup d'œil sur la XXVIe Biennale de Venise,* Cahiers d'Art, 1952, 27, pp. 237-287. — T. Lundgren, *Biennalen och Värlaskonsten,* Konstrevy, 1952, pp. 208-215. — B. Meyers, *From Cubism to Industrial Arts,* American Artist, 1952, No. 2, pp. 40-43, 71-73. — G. H. Hamilton, *Anonyme no longer,* Art News, 1952-1953, No. 9, pp. 36-37, 58-60. — G. Buffet, *La "Section d'Or",* Art d'Aujourd'hui, 1953, No. 3-4, pp. 74-76. — J. Laude, *Le monde du cirque et ses jeux,* Revue d'Esthétique, 1953, VI, pp. 411-433. — W. Schmalenbach, *Zur Funktion der modernen Kunst,* Werk, 1953, pp. 416-428. — D. V., *Fernand Léger, sculptures polychromes en céramique,* Cahiers d'Art, 1953, 28, I, pp. 151-153. — J. E. Brown, *Fernand Léger: "Man and Woman",* Bulletin of the Art Association, Indianapolis 1953, No. 1, pp. 21-24. — J. CASSOU, *Développement de l'art de Fernand Léger*, Revue des Arts, 1953, III, pp. 40-43. — R. VAN GINDERTAEL, *Notes en marge de quelques dessins cubistes*, Art d'Aujourd'hui, 1953, No. 3-4, pp. 63-69. — C. ZERVOS, *La Situation faite au dessin dans l'art contemporain*, Cahiers d'Art, 1953, 28, pp. 161-181. — F. ELGAR, *Léger plus religieux que Rouault!*, Carrefour, April 15, 1953. — U. BINDER-HAGELSTANGE, *Kubistische Theaterdekorationen*, Kunstwerk, 1953, No. 1, pp. 12-23. — K. KUH, *New Sculpture at the Art Institute*, Art Institute of Chicago Quarterly, 1953, 47, pp. 62-66. — J. MARCENAC, *La grande parade du travail et du génie*, Les Lettres françaises, November 11, 1954, p. 10. — G. PEILLEX, *L'église de Courfaivre a demandé des vitraux à Fernand Léger*, Art-Documents, 1954, No. 45, pp. 3 and 9. — B. DORIVAL, *Musée d'Art moderne. Nouvelles acquisitions*, Revue des Arts, 1954, IV, pp. 171-174. — J. MELLQUIST, *Essai dialectique sur la XXVIIᵉ Biennale de Venise*, Arts Plastiques, September 1954, pp. 22-38. — H. HILDEBRANDT, *Wandmalerei*, Kunstwerk, 1954, No. 5, pp. 3-30. — J. RICHARDSON, *Au château des cubistes*, L'Œil, 1955, No. 4, pp. 19-22. — *Les Expositions. Groupe Espace*, Aujour d'hui, 1955, No. 4, pp. 20-23. — *La vie d'un peintre*, L'Œil, 1955, No. 10, pp. 40-44. — R. COGNIAT, *Litografie a colori*, Biennale di Venezia, 1955, No. 23, pp. 13-14. — B. KOCHNO, *Le ballet et le peintre*, Graphis, 1955, pp. 352-359. — M. R. CAPELLADES and L. E. JUILLERAT, *L'originalité iconographique des vitraux de Courfaivre*, Pour l'Art, 1955, No. 44, pp. 13-21, 26-28. — GÉO-CHARLES, *Fernand Léger*, Courrier graphique, 1955, No. 79, pp. 21-29. — D. COOPER, *La grande parade de F. Léger*, L'Œil, 1955, No. 1, pp. 21-26. — E. TRIER, *Der späte Léger*, Kunstwerk, 1955, No. 2, p. 31. — *Hommage à F. Léger, peintures de 1920 à 1930*, Derrière le Miroir, 1955, No. 79-81. — G. CHARENSOL, *Fernand Léger*, Revue des Deux Mondes, 1955, V, pp. 713-722. — B. URBANOWICZ, *Fernand Léger*, Prz. Artyst., 1955, No. 3-4, pp. 3-23. — A. T. SCHOENER, *Gleizes*, The Cincinnati Art Museum Bulletin, March 1956, p. 21. — J. LASSAIGNE, *F. Léger*, Prisme des Arts, 1956, No. 4, p. 25. — M. JARDOT, *Fernand Léger, 1881-1955*, Quadrum, 1956, No. 2, p. 199. — D. H. KAHNWEILER, *Entretiens avec Picasso*, Quadrum, 1956, No. 2, p. 76. — P. DESCARGUES, *La leçon de Léger*, Les Lettres françaises, June 14, 1956, p. 12. — A. DE RIDDER, *Charley Toorop, Fernand Léger, Maurice Utrillo*, Brussels 1956, pp. 8-15. — F. MATHEY, *Situation du vitrail en France*, Quadrum, 1957, pp. 93-97. — L. ARAGON, *Léger parmi nous*, Les Lettres françaises, No. 766, March 26, 1959, pp. 1, 14. — *Le Musée Fernand Léger à Biot*, Aujourd'hui, 1959, No. 22, pp. 57-59. — P. FRANCASTEL, *Il Futurismo e il suo tempo*, La Biennale, 1959, 36-37, pp. 3-5. — M. CALVESI, *Il Futurismo e l'avanguardia europea*, La Biennale, 1959, 36-37, p. 27. — G. ARISTARCO, *Teoria futurista e film d'avanguardia*, La Biennale, 1959, 36-37, p. 85. — G. SADOUL, *Fernand Léger ou la cinéplastique*, Cinéma 59, Paris 1959, No. 35, pp. 73-82. — A. JOUFFROY, *Biographie*, Le Jardin des Arts, April 1960, pp. 58-59. — L. HOCTIN, *Folkwang Museum, Essen*, L'Œil, July-August, 1960, p. 30. — M. RAGON,

Peinture en mouvement et sculpture animée dans le ballet contemporain, Cimaise, 1960, No. 47, pp. 17, 22-24. — F. A. VIALLET, *La fin du tableau?,* Cimaise, 1960, No. 49, pp. 24, 28. — J. L. FERRIER, *Le musée Léger,* Les Temps modernes, 1960, No. 172, pp. 169-177. — J. AUDIBERTI, *Rouge,* Nouvelle Revue française, 1960, No. 96, pp. 1002-1008. — L. ARAGON, *Fernand Léger. La Seine-et-Oise,* poem, Les Lettres françaises, 1960, No. 854, p. 1. — R. J. MOULIN, *Une typographie dans l'esprit de Léger,* Les Lettres françaises, 1960, No. 854, p. 12. — P. STERCKX, *Art et Machines,* Journal des Arts Plastiques, Brussels, 1961. — N., *Das Léger-Museum in Biot zeugt von des Künstlers Anliegen: Der Mensch und seine Arbeit,* Die Woche, Olten 1961, No. 18, pp. 13-15. — J. MEURIS, *Les beaux-arts et la machine,* Industrie, Brussels, May 1961, p. 287.

Special Issues of Periodicals

Sélection, Antwerp 1929, articles by B. CENDRARS *(Construction),* W. GEORGE *(Léger et les objets dans l'espace),* E. TÉRIADE *(Nord-Sud),* P. MORAND *(Le développement de F. Léger),* M. RAYNAL *(L'influence de Léger sur l'art décoratif),* FLOUQUET *(L'humanité dans l'œuvre de Léger),* T. VAN DOESBURG *(Léger et le cubisme),* LE CORBUSIER *(L'architecture et Fernand Léger),* B. CENDRARS *(Modernités),* poem by R. GUIETTE *(Escalier).* — *Cahiers d'Art,* 1933, 3-4, pp. 85-172, articles by ZERVOS *(Léger est-il cubiste?),* APOLLINAIRE, A. SALMON, E. LAUGIER, OZENFANT, J. H. LEVESQUE, O. MOLL, P. FIERENS, I. EHRENBOURG, H. HEILMEIER, R. HOPPE, Darius MILHAUD, P. COURTHION, J. J. SWEENEY, Waldemar GEORGE, C. EINSTEIN, BULLIET, M. RAYNAL, T. VAN DOESBURG, G. BAZIN, poem by B. CENDRARS. — *Les Lettres françaises,* No. 582, August 25, 1955, *Hommage à Fernand Léger:* articles by L. ARAGON *(Le sourire de Léger),* R. BRICE *(Léger et la céramique),* J. CASSOU *(Le poète de notre âge industriel),* D. COOPER *(Un langage),* P. DESCARGUES *(La guerre de 14),* M. JARDOT *(Antiromantisme et gentillesse),* M. LEIRIS *(Le savoir-vivre d'un créateur),* MAIAKOVSKI *(Léger),* G. SADOUL *("J'ai failli abandonner la peinture pour le cinéma"),* etc.

INDEX

139

LIST OF COLORPLATES

TABLE OF CONTENTS

THIS, THE THIRTY-EIGHTH VOLUME OF "THE TASTE OF OUR
TIME" SERIES, WAS PRODUCED BY THE TECHNICAL STAFF
OF EDITIONS D'ART ALBERT SKIRA. FINISHED THE THIRTIETH
DAY OF AUGUST, NINETEEN HUNDRED AND SIXTY-TWO.

TEXT AND ILLUSTRATIONS BY

COLOR STUDIOS

IMPRIMERIES RÉUNIES, LAUSANNE.

PLATES ENGRAVED BY GUEZELLE & RENOUARD, PARIS.

PHOTOGRAPHS BY

*Adrion, Paris (pages 92, 106), Maurice Babey, Olten (pages 20, 23, 43, 51, 52,
63, 67, 72, 75, 77, 86, 88, 94, 96, 99, 104, 109, 118), Henry B. Beville, Washington
(pages 26, 32, 36, 46, 69, 78, 98, 110, 113, 114), Doisneau-Rapho, Paris (page 112),
Claudio Emmer, Milan (page 29), Hans Hinz, Basel (page 37), Halbach, Ratingen
(pages 50, 82), Louis Laniepce, Paris (pages 3, 30, 34, 47, 107), Meyer, Vienna
(page 40), Rainbow, Paris (page 64), Editions Skira, Geneva (pages 56, 61, 70,
85, 101), and by courtesy of the Museum of Modern Art, New York (page 62),
the Musée Fernand Léger, Biot (page 91), and the Stedelijk Museum, Amsterdam
(page 54).*

PRINTED IN SWITZERLAND